AF716784

STRATEGIC FUNDAMENTALS OF VULNERABILITY MANAGEMENT FOR IT CYBERSECURITY ANALYSTS

BY

AUGUSTINE E. ETA, PH.D

Copyright Page

© 2025 **Augustine Eta**

All rights reserved.

No part of this publication may be reproduced, stored in a retrieval system, or transmitted in any form or by any means—electronic, mechanical, photocopying, recording, or otherwise—without the prior written permission of the publisher, except in the case of brief quotations embodied in critical articles or reviews.

Published by Royal Book House

www.royalbookhouse.com

Cover design by Royal Book House

Edited and proofread by the Royal Book House

ISBN: [Insert ISBN]

Printed in the United States of America

First Edition

This book is a work of nonfiction. All historical references, citations, and interpretations are based on publicly available sources and the author's original analysis. Any resemblance to real persons in fictionalized examples is purely coincidental.

For permissions, inquiries, or speaking engagements, please contact:

etawisdombooks@gmail.com

Contents

Dedication. 1

Acknowledgment 2

About the Author. 3

Introduction 5

Chapter One 9

What is Cybersecurity, IT Security, and Information Systems Security? 9

The CIA Triad: Core Principles of Security 10

What Is Confidentiality? 11

What Is Integrity in Cybersecurity?. 13

What Is Availability in Cybersecurity?. 14

Chapter Two 18

Foundations of Vulnerability Management 18

Background, Definition, and Scope of Vulnerability Management 18

Insecure or Untracked IoT Devices 24

Insider Threats & Human Error. 24

Detecting Vulnerabilities Proactively. 25
Auditing Network Assets 25
Identifying Security Vulnerabilities: Penetration Testing 25
Building a Threat Intelligence Framework 26
Definition of Vulnerability Management 27
Scope of Vulnerability Management 27
Strategic Importance. 27
Key terminology and lifecycle stages 29
The Role of Vulnerability Management in Cybersecurity Programs 33
Core Role in Cybersecurity Programs 33
Value to Cybersecurity Maturity. 35
Strategic Takeaway. 35
Chapter Three **36**
Risk-Based Prioritization 36
Understanding Risk vs. Severity 36
Understanding Risk 37
Risk ≠ Severity. 37
Strategic Integration 38
CVSS Scoring and Business Impact Analysis 38
CVSS (Common Vulnerability Scoring System) 38
CVSS Structure. 39

Business Impact Analysis (BIA) 40

Aligning Priorities with Organizational Risk Appetite 42

What Is Risk Appetite? 42

Strategic Outcome 44

Chapter Four... 45

Vulnerability Assessment Tools 45

Overview Of Leading Tools: Nessus, Qualys, Rapid7 Insight vm, Splunk 45

3. Rapid7 Insight VM 47

Tool Selection Criteria 49

Deployment and Integration with SIEM and CMDB 52

Chapter Five... 56

Asset Discovery and Inventory 56

The Importance of Accurate Asset Inventories 56

Passive vs. Active Discovery Methods 58

Integrating Asset Data with Scan Strategies 60

Chapter Six 66

Scan Strategy and Scheduling. 66

Choosing Scan Types: Authenticated vs. Unauthenticated 66

Scheduling Scans for Coverage and Minimal Disruption 68

Handling Sensitive Systems and Legacy Environments 71

Chapter Seven 77
Vulnerability Classification and Validation 77
Differentiating False Positives and Actionable Findings 77
Categorizing Vulnerabilities 79
Exploitability Assessment and Threat Intelligence Integration 81
Chapter Eight 86
Remediation and Exception Handling 86
Creating Effective Remediation Plans 86
Core Components of a Remediation Plan 86
Cross-Functional Coordination with IT Operations 89
Managing Exceptions and Documenting Risk Acceptance 91
Chapter Nine 94
Compliance and Regulatory Alignment 94
Mapping Findings to Frameworks (NIST SP 800-53, ISO 27001, FISMA) 94
Reporting for Audits and Compliance Assessments 96
Demonstrating Continuous Improvement 100
Chapter Ten 107
Metrics, Dashboards, and Reporting 107
KPIs and Metrics in Cybersecurity 107
Building Executive-Level Dashboards 110
Reporting to Technical vs. Business Audiences 115

Chapter Eleven **118**
Program Maturity and Continuous Improvement 118
Assessing Program Maturity with CMMI 118
Automation and Orchestration Opportunities 119
Incorporating Lessons Learned 121
APPENDIX A 126
APPENDIX B 128
APPENDIX C 133
APPENDIX D 142
APPENDIX E 146
APPENDIX F 148
APPENDIX G 150
APPENDIX H 152
APPENDIX I 155
APPENDIX J 158
APPENDIX K 163
APPENDIX L 166
APPENDIX M 170
APPENDIX N 175
APPENDIX O 178
APPENDIX P 183

APPENDIX Q 189
APPENDIX R 193
APPENDIX S. 197
APPENDIX T 201
APPENDIX U 207
INDEX 214

Dedication

This book is lovingly dedicated to my father, Michael Etta Ayuk, of blessed memory. He raised me in the reverent fear of the Lord and instilled in me a deep respect for hard work. A lion-hearted man, he lived with unwavering courage and strength.

Acknowledgment

I am deeply grateful to **Royal Book House** for their outstanding editorial expertise and unwavering commitment to excellence in the publication of *Strategic Fundamentals of Vulnerability Management for IT Cybersecurity Analysts*. Their meticulous editing and proofreading significantly enhanced the clarity, coherence, and scholarly rigor of this work.

Special appreciation goes to **Aston Young**, whose consistent updates, timely communication, and professional coordination throughout the editing and formatting process were invaluable. His attentiveness and reliability ensured a smooth and efficient workflow, allowing this manuscript to reach completion with precision and care.

To the editors and proofreaders whose expertise shaped this book's final presentation, thank you for your dedication and for upholding the highest standards of publishing. To all who contributed to this endeavor, I extend my sincere gratitude for your commitment to quality and your belief in the vision behind this book.

About the Author

Dr. **Augustine Eta** is a cybersecurity professional with a Ph.D. in Organizational Leadership and a Master of Science in Information Technology, specializing in Homeland Security Management. His career reflects a passion for integrating technology, security, and leadership to safeguard digital infrastructures, drive innovation, and foster organizational growth.

With over 15 years of experience, he has developed expertise in vulnerability management, enterprise risk assessment, threat analysis, and continuous monitoring. He is proficient in leading platforms such as **Splunk, Nessus, Tanium,** and **Microsoft Defender**. He also provides expert leadership in Cyber Hygiene and High-Value Assets vulnerability management, ensuring data validation, accuracy, and timely reporting.

His knowledge extends across a wide range of compliance and security standards, including **FISMA, NIST, ISO 27001, PCI DSS, CIS, HIPAA, SOX, HITRUST,** and **OMB**, with a strong emphasis on IT infrastructure protection.

Beyond his technical expertise, Dr. Augustine is also an accomplished author. His book *Organizational Leadership Essentials: An Academic Analysis* provides a comprehensive exploration of leadership principles.

In addition, he serves on the boards of two non-profits, leading one as president.

He holds multiple certifications, including **Certified in Cybersecurity (CC), Certified Information Security Manager (CISM), Certified Information Systems Auditor (CISA), Project Manager Accredited Certification,** and **Scrum Master Certification.** These credentials reflect his commitment to addressing emerging challenges in cybersecurity, compliance, and risk management.

Introduction

Strategic Fundamentals of Vulnerability Management for the IT Cybersecurity Analyst

In today's hyperconnected digital landscape, **vulnerability management has evolved from a technical function to a strategic imperative.** As cyber threats increase in both sophistication and scale, organizations must adopt **proactive, risk-informed approaches** to protect their assets, safeguard sensitive data, and preserve reputation.

This book is designed to equip **IT cybersecurity analysts** with the foundational knowledge, practical tools, and strategic mindset necessary to **build, operate, and mature a robust vulnerability management program.** Whether you are a new analyst entering the field or a seasoned professional refining your methods, this guide provides a **comprehensive roadmap** that integrates technical execution with governance-level insight, aligning vulnerability practices with organizational objectives and regulatory demands.

We begin by clarifying the essential distinctions between **cybersecurity, IT security, and information security**, anchored in the timeless **CIA Triad: Confidentiality, Integrity, and Availability**. From there, the text progresses through the full lifecycle of vulnerability management, demonstrating how vulnerabilities are identified, assessed, prioritized, and remediated in modern enterprise environments.

The chapters unfold systematically:

- **Chapter 1** establishes the foundational concepts of cybersecurity, IT security, and information security through the lens of the CIA Triad.
- **Chapter 2** defines the scope and lifecycle of vulnerability management, situating it within broader cybersecurity programs.
- **Chapter 3** explores **risk-based prioritization**, distinguishing between risk and severity, and introduces CVSS scoring, business impact analysis, and alignment with organizational risk appetite.
- **Chapter 4** offers a comparative overview of leading tools—such as **Nessus, Qualys, and Rapid7 InsightVM**—and provides guidance for integration with platforms like SIEM and CMDB.
- **Chapter 5** emphasizes **asset discovery and inventory**, comparing active and passive methods for informing scan strategies.
- **Chapter 6** focuses on scan strategies and scheduling, covering authenticated vs. unauthenticated scans and approaches for sensitive or legacy systems.
- **Chapter 7** addresses **classification and validation**, guiding analysts on differentiating false positives from actionable findings and leveraging threat intelligence.

- **Chapter 8** explores **remediation and exception handling**, including cross-team coordination, remediation planning, and documented risk acceptance.
- **Chapter 9** aligns vulnerability management with compliance frameworks such as **NIST 800-53, ISO 27001, and FISMA**, providing strategies for audit readiness and continuous improvement.
- **Chapter 10** introduces **metrics, dashboards, and reporting**, equipping analysts to tailor KPIs and executive dashboards for both technical and leadership audiences.
- **Chapter 11** provides a roadmap for **program maturity**, drawing from CMMI models and highlighting automation, orchestration, AI-driven scanning, and cloud-native security.
- The **appendix and index** serve as extended references, mapping key compliance frameworks—including **GDPR, PCI DSS, SOX, and FedRAMP**—alongside foundational network concepts such as the **OSI model, core protocols, and critical ports.**
- In sum, this book is both a **practical guide and authoritative reference,** designed to empower cybersecurity professionals with the **knowledge, tools, and foresight** required to establish resilient vulnerability management programs in today's rapidly evolving IT environments.

Vulnerability
Management
Lifecycle
Discover
Prioritize
Assess
Report
Remediate
Verify

Chapter One

What is Cybersecurity, IT Security, and Information Systems Security?

Cybersecurity is the practice of protecting digital systems, networks, and data from unauthorized access, attacks, or damage. It focuses on defending against threats such as malware, phishing, ransomware, and hacking attempts.

- **Scope:** Primarily digital environments (e.g., internet, cloud, endpoints)
- **Goal:** Prevent, detect, and respond to cyber threats
- **Example:** Using firewalls and antivirus software to block malicious traffic

IT Security (Information Technology Security) is a broader discipline that includes cybersecurity but also covers physical and administrative safeguards for IT infrastructure.

- **Scope:** Digital and physical IT assets (servers, networks, devices)

- **Goal:** Protect systems and data from unauthorized access or disruption
- **Example:** Securing server rooms with access controls and monitoring software

Security Information Systems (INFOSEC) focuses on protecting information—whether digital, physical, or spoken—from unauthorized access, alteration, or destruction.

- **Scope:** All forms of information (digital files, paper documents, verbal communication)
- **Goal:** Ensure confidentiality, integrity, and availability of information
- **Example:** Encrypting sensitive files and implementing access policies

The CIA Triad: Core Principles of Security

The **CIA Triad** is a foundational model in information security, representing three key principles:

Principle	Description	Example Use Case
Confidentiality	Ensuring that information is accessible only to authorized individuals	Encrypting emails to protect sensitive data
Integrity	Maintaining the accuracy and trustworthiness of data	Using checksums to detect file tampering

Availability	Ensuring that authorized users can access data and systems when needed	Implementing redundant servers for uptime

What Is Confidentiality?

Confidentiality refers to ensuring that sensitive information is accessible only to those authorized to view it. It is one of the three pillars of the CIA Triad and is foundational to protecting privacy, intellectual property, and national security.

Key Objectives:

- Prevent unauthorized disclosure of data
- Protect personal, financial, medical, and proprietary information
- Comply with legal and regulatory standards (e.g., HIPAA, FISMA, GDPR)

How Confidentiality Is Ensured:

1. **Encryption** – Converts data into an unreadable format unless decrypted with a key. Used for data at rest (e.g., files, databases) and in transit (e.g., emails, VPN traffic).
2. **Access Control** – Role-based access (RBAC), attribute-based access (ABAC), and mandatory access control (MAC) ensure users only access data necessary for their role.
3. **Authentication & Authorization** – Multifactor authentication (MFA), biometrics, and smart cards verify identity before granting access.

4. **Data Masking & Tokenization** – Obscures sensitive data for testing or analytics; tokenization replaces sensitive data with nonsensitive equivalents.
5. **Security Policies & Training** – Clear data handling procedures and regular awareness training to prevent social engineering and phishing.
6. **Network Security Controls** – Firewalls, intrusion prevention systems (IPS), and secure protocols (e.g., TLS/SSL) prevent unauthorized access to data in transit.
7. **Data Loss Prevention (DLP)** – Monitors and restricts data movement to prevent leaks; can block emails, uploads, or transfers containing sensitive content.
8. **Physical Security** – Locked server rooms, surveillance, and badge access prevent unauthorized physical entry.

Real-World Example:

A healthcare provider storing patient records may use:

- Encryption to protect records in the database
- Access controls to ensure only medical staff can view them
- MFA to prevent unauthorized logins
- DLP to block external emailing of patient data
- Training to help staff recognize phishing attempts

What Is Integrity in Cybersecurity?

Integrity ensures that data remains accurate, complete, and unaltered from its original or intended state. It guarantees that information is trustworthy—whether stored, transmitted, or processed—and that changes are authorized, traceable, and intentional.

Why Integrity Matters:

- Prevents unauthorized modifications to critical data
- Supports auditability and regulatory compliance
- Enables trustworthy decision-making based on reliable information
- Protects against silent manipulation (e.g., altered logs, tampered transactions)

How Integrity Can Be Ensured:

1. **Cryptographic Hashing** – Generates a unique fingerprint of data (e.g., SHA256). Any change alters the hash, signaling tampering.
2. **Digital Signatures** – Combines hashing with encryption to verify authenticity and integrity.
3. **Access Controls** – Role-based access (RBAC) and least privilege prevent unauthorized data changes.
4. **Audit Logs & Change Tracking** – Records who accessed or modified data, when, and how.
5. **Version Control Systems** – Tracks changes over time, allowing rollback to previous versions.

6. **Checksums & Parity Checks** – Validate data integrity during transfer or storage.
7. **Backup & Recovery Plans** – Preserve unaltered copies for restoration.
8. **Intrusion Detection Systems (IDS)** – Monitor for unauthorized changes or anomalies.

Common Threats to Integrity:

- **Man-in-the-Middle Attacks:** Alter data in transit
- **Insider Misuse:** Unauthorized changes to records
- **Malware & Ransomware:** Corrupt or encrypt data
- **Human Error:** Accidental deletion or misconfiguration
- **SQL Injection:** Unauthorized database manipulation

Framework Alignment:

Control Area	**NIST SP 800-53**	**ISO/IEC 27001:2022**
Data Integrity	SI7, AU6, SC12	A.8.7, A.12.2.1
Access Control	AC2, AC6	A.5.15, A.8.2
Audit & Monitoring	CA7, AU2	A.5.9, A.12.4.1
Backup & Recovery	CP9, CP10	A.17.1.3, A.17.2.1

What Is Availability in Cybersecurity?

Availability ensures that authorized users can reliably access systems, data, and services when needed—without disruption. If integrity is about trust and confidentiality is about privacy, availability is about dependability.

Why Availability Matters:

- Supports business continuity and operational resilience
- Enables timely decision-making and service delivery
- Prevents downtime-related financial, reputational, and legal losses
- Ensures access to critical systems during emergencies

How Availability Can Be Ensured:

1. **Redundancy & Failover Systems** – Duplicate hardware, network paths, and services with automatic failover. Examples: RAID arrays, high availability clusters, load balancers.
2. **Disaster Recovery & Business Continuity Plans** – Define recovery time (RTO) and recovery point (RPO) objectives, with offsite backups and cloud replication.
3. **Regular Maintenance & Patch Management** – Prevent outages from bugs or vulnerabilities.
4. **DDoS Protection & Traffic Filtering** – Use firewalls, rate limiting, and anti-DoS services; monitor for abnormal traffic spikes.
5. **Cloud Scalability & Elastic Resources** – Automatically scale to meet demand, using distributed architectures to avoid single points of failure.
6. **Monitoring & Alerting Systems** – Real-time health checks and alerts to detect and prevent outages.

7. **Access Control & Authentication** – Prevent unauthorized access that could disrupt services.
8. **Use multifactor authentication (MFA)** and implement robust session management to prevent unauthorized access that could compromise availability.

Common Threats to Availability

Threat Type	Impact
DDoS Attacks	Overwhelm systems, causing service outages.
Hardware Failures	Downtime caused by physical component breakdown.
Ransomware	Locks access to systems and data.
Natural Disasters	Damage infrastructure and disrupt operations.
Software Bugs	Cause crashes, memory leaks, or instability.
Insider Sabotage	Intentional disruption by privileged users.

Framework Alignment

Control Area	NIST SP 800-53	ISO/IEC 27001:2022
System Availability	CP2, CP9, SC5	A.17.1.1, A.17.2.1
Incident Response	IR4, IR8	A.5.24, A.5.25
Monitoring & Resilience	AU6, SI4	A.12.4.1, A.12.1.3
Redundancy & Recovery	CP10, PE9	A.17.1.3, A.11.1.4

Diagram of the Vulnerability Management Lifecycle — visualizing the complete flow from discovery to continuous improvement — *coming soon.*

Chapter Two

Foundations of Vulnerability Management

Background, Definition, and Scope of Vulnerability Management

Vulnerability management is a cornerstone of modern cybersecurity, crucial for identifying, assessing, and mitigating weaknesses that attackers could exploit. Here is a comprehensive breakdown of its definition and scope:

Background

In our current digital landscape, every business faces constant exposure to threats—regardless of its size or industry. From global giants in the Fortune 500 to neighborhood storefronts, no organization is immune to cyber risks. The reality is stark: the sheer volume of threats makes it impossible to stop them all.

According to cybersecurity firm Kaspersky Lab, its threat detection technologies processed **360,000 new malicious files daily in 2017.** That translates to approximately **250 new malware variants emerging every minute.**

And malware is just one piece of the puzzle. Businesses also contend with cybersecurity threats and system vulnerabilities that malicious actors could exploit to steal sensitive data or disrupt operations.

A **vulnerability** in computer security refers to a weakness or flaw in a system, network, or application that can be exploited. These gaps could allow attackers to gain unauthorized access, manipulate operations, or cause damage.

This differs from a **cyber threat**, which typically involves external risks such as a malware campaign, phishing attempt, or hostile actor targeting systems. While threats are external, vulnerabilities are inherent to the systems. Attackers do not intentionally place vulnerabilities, yet cybercriminals actively seek and leverage them to launch exploits, leading some to conflate the terms.

The method of exploitation depends on the specific vulnerability and the attacker's goals. Vulnerabilities can stem from poor configurations, outdated software, unintended software interactions, or flawed code development. The following are common causes of vulnerabilities in an enterprise:

Malware

The creation of new malware continues at a staggering pace. Yet, while figures like **360,000 new malware samples per day** may seem overwhelming, it is essential to recognize that many of these are modified versions of existing malware—designed to evade detection by altering key attributes just enough to bypass antivirus filters.

Over time, a wide array of malware types has emerged, each with distinct methods of compromising systems:

- **Ransomware:** Encrypts a victim's files or entire storage drives, locking users out of their data. Attackers then demand a ransom in exchange for the decryption key. If the victim refuses to pay, the key may be destroyed, resulting in permanent data loss.
- **Trojans:** Named after the deceptive wooden horse in Greek mythology, Trojans disguise themselves as legitimate applications to trick users into installing them. Once embedded, they bypass frontline security measures and can deliver various malicious payloads.
- **Worms:** These self-replicating programs spread autonomously through networks, often via email. Once inside a system, a worm may access a user's contacts or file-sharing services and propagate itself further, usually impersonating the victim to avoid detection.
- Some sophisticated malware variants go beyond infiltration by **silently exfiltrating sensitive information** to designated ports or external servers controlled by attackers.

Defense Against Malware

While basic antivirus tools provide a foundational layer of defense, comprehensive protection requires a **layered security approach**. This includes:

- Next-generation firewalls with deep packet inspection
- Intrusion detection systems (IDS)
- Advanced email filtering
- Regular cybersecurity awareness training for employees

By combining technical defenses with ongoing employee education, organizations can build stronger resilience against evolving malware threats.

Unpatched Security Vulnerabilities

Despite new threats, many cyberattacks still rely on exploiting **known, longstanding vulnerabilities.** Failure to address these weaknesses—whether due to oversight or inconvenience—can leave systems exposed.

Users often dismiss "update available" notifications, viewing them as interruptions rather than essential maintenance. Yet skipping a routine update can lead to exploits that cost organizations far more in downtime, remediation, and reputational damage.

The solution is straightforward: establish a **consistent update schedule.** Designate a day each week for your IT team to check and apply the latest patches across systems, applications, and firmware. This simple discipline remains one of the most effective measures against preventable attacks.

Hidden Backdoor Programs

Backdoors are intentionally placed mechanisms that allow remote access to a computer or network—often for legitimate reasons such as technical support or diagnostics. However, when these programs are embedded without user knowledge or are poorly secured, they become serious vulnerabilities.

Hidden backdoors pose significant risks, particularly when exploited by individuals with unauthorized access. Once discovered, these gateways can be used to infiltrate the compromised device and potentially the wider network it connects to.

Identifying and remediating hidden backdoors requires **thorough system audits** and the use of endpoint detection tools capable of uncovering anomalies that may be missed by conventional security scans.

Hidden Backdoors in Networking Equipment

A notable case reported by *Bloomberg* revealed that critical vulnerabilities were embedded in Huawei's home internet routers. According to the article, **Vodafone**—Europe's largest telecommunications provider—identified covert backdoors within Huawei's software that could have enabled unauthorized access to its fixed-line infrastructure in Italy, affecting millions of homes and businesses.

Vodafone initially requested the removal of the backdoors in 2011 and received assurances from Huawei that the issue was resolved. However, subsequent evaluations indicated that the vulnerabilities remained, posing significant risks if exploited by threat actors.

Excessive Privileges via Superuser/Admin Accounts

Minimizing user access is a cornerstone of effective vulnerability management. Yet many organizations fall short by granting broad administrative privileges across the network. In some cases, misconfigured systems even allow standard users to create or elevate accounts to admin status—creating dangerous pathways for compromise.

Ensuring that every account has access only to the resources essential for its role—and restricting the creation of privileged accounts—is vital for reducing internal attack surfaces.

Automatic Script Execution Without Security Validation

Certain browsers, such as older versions of Safari, have default behaviors that automatically execute files marked as "safe." Threat actors exploit this by crafting malicious code that imitates trusted scripts, enabling it to run without user awareness.

Disabling **autorun features** for unverified scripts—particularly in line with the **CIS Apple OS benchmark**—is an essential safeguard that goes beyond simply blocking suspicious websites.

Undetected Software Bugs & Integration Conflicts

As software systems grow more complex and interconnected, vulnerabilities become harder to predict. Even isolated **applications** may contain bugs that create security holes. When applications interact or integrate, the risks multiply—unanticipated code behaviors, logic conflicts, and permission misalignments can open new paths for exploitation.

Attackers actively hunt for these flaws, making **secure coding practices** and rigorous interoperability testing critical components of a defensive strategy.

Phishing & Social Engineering Exploits

Phishing attacks continue to pose significant threats, relying on **psychological manipulation** rather than technological force. Emails impersonating trusted vendors or internal personnel often prompt recipients to download malware or surrender credentials under false pretenses. To counter these attacks, organizations should implement:

- **Email Scanners** to flag and quarantine malicious attachments
- **Multifactor Authentication** (MFA) to make credentials harder to misuse

- **Cybersecurity Awareness Training** to equip employees to recognize red flags
- **Defense-in-Depth Architectures** to segment systems and contain breaches
- **Least Privilege Access Controls** to minimize exposure if an account is compromised

Insecure or Untracked IoT Devices

The growing use of Internet of Things (IoT) technologies introduces a swarm of often-overlooked endpoints—smart printers, appliances, cameras, and more. Each device represents a potential entry point for attackers, especially if it operates with default credentials or is not included in routine security sweeps.

Conducting regular asset audits to inventory devices and their software environments ensures IoT components are monitored, patched, and integrated into the organization's overall security framework.

Insider Threats & Human Error

Employees remain one of the most unpredictable variables in cybersecurity. Whether intentional (e.g., privilege abuse) or accidental (e.g., clicking a malicious link), internal users often cause breaches. Reinforcing cybersecurity hygiene through awareness training, enforcing least privilege, and applying technical controls such as activity monitoring helps mitigate both malicious and inadvertent threats.

Detecting Vulnerabilities Proactively

Identifying vulnerabilities before attackers do is essential—but many organizations struggle without proper tools or processes. Begin by:

Auditing Network Assets

Create a comprehensive inventory of all devices, operating systems, and applications in use. This helps flag obsolete platforms or known vulnerabilities tied to specific versions.

Without this visibility, organizations may assume full coverage while running outdated or unpatched systems. For instance, as cited in *The New York Times*, a JPMorgan Chase breach occurred when one server was left out of a two-factor authentication upgrade, making it a gateway for attackers.

Identifying Security Vulnerabilities: Penetration Testing

Once an organization has audited its network and cataloged every asset, the next step is to simulate real-world attacks through penetration testing. This "stress test" helps uncover security gaps before adversaries exploit them.

Penetration testing methodologies vary based on an organization's architecture and risk appetite—there is no universal approach. However, standard practices often include:

1. Engaging a certified ethical hacker ("white hat") to perform testing during a defined window.
2. Reviewing systems and configurations for known vulnerabilities and outdated components.

3. Launching simulated attacks to assess whether potential weaknesses can be exploited or to uncover previously unknown flaws.
4. Activating the organization's incident response plan (IRP) to test how effectively the team can detect, contain, and remediate threats.
5. Importantly, penetration testing not only exposes technical vulnerabilities but also reveals operational weaknesses in response protocols, influencing improvements to policies, playbooks, and staff readiness.

Building a Threat Intelligence Framework

While penetration testing is invaluable, it should be complemented by a robust threat intelligence framework—a proactive model for staying ahead of evolving cyber threats.

- A sound framework enables organizations to:
- Clarify protection priorities (e.g., sensitive data, customer-facing systems)
- Define strategic security goals
- Profile key threat actors and sources
- Adapt defenses based on known and emerging tactics
- Integrate curated threat feeds to gain visibility into global cyber trends

Due to the complexity and resource demands of building such a framework, many businesses partner with Managed Security Services Providers (MSSPs). These expert providers offer:

- Advanced penetration testing and continuous vulnerability assessments
- Support for building or refining IRPs and security policies
- Access to up-to-date threat intelligence sources tailored to your industry

Understanding your most pressing threat exposures is the foundation of sound cybersecurity governance. But maintaining vigilance—and continuously adapting defenses—requires expertise, foresight, and a commitment to improvement.

Definition of Vulnerability Management

Vulnerability management is a continuous, proactive, and structured process for identifying, evaluating, treating, and reporting security vulnerabilities in systems, applications, networks, and devices. The goal is to reduce an organization's attack surface and ensure systems remain resilient against evolving threats.

It is not a one-time activity but a lifecycle that integrates with broader risk management and IT operations, ideally aligning with frameworks like NIST CSF, ISO 27001, or FISMA.

Scope of Vulnerability Management

The scope extends across several dimensions and domains within an organization:

1. **Asset Coverage**
   • Physical infrastructure: servers, desktops, routers, switches
   • Virtual and cloud environments: VMs, containers, SaaS platforms

+ Applications: web apps, mobile apps, ERP systems
+ Endpoint devices: laptops, smartphones, IoT sensors

2. **Vulnerability Types**
   + Software flaws (e.g., buffer overflows, code injection)
   + Configuration issues (e.g., default credentials, misconfigured firewalls)
   + Missing patches (outdated systems not running the latest security updates)
   + Unsecured services (e.g., open ports, exposed APIs)
   + Third-party component vulnerabilities (e.g., outdated libraries, plugins)
3. **Tools and Techniques**
   + Vulnerability scanners: Nessus, Qualys, Rapid7 InsightVM
   + Threat intelligence platforms: Recorded Future, Mandiant
   + SIEM/SOAR integrations: for alerting, triage, and remediation workflows
   + Configuration management systems: ServiceNow, Tanium, Ansible
4. **Processes Included**
   + Asset inventory and classification
   + Scheduled vulnerability scans (authenticated/unauthenticated)
   + Risk-based prioritization (CVSS + business impact)
   + Patch management and remediation coordination
   + Reporting, metrics, and executive dashboards
   + Exception handling and compensating control documentation
   + Audit readiness and regulatory compliance
5. **Regulatory and Compliance Relevance**
   + NIST SP 800-53: maps vulnerability activities to controls like RA5, SI2, and CM6
   + FISMA: requires federal agencies to monitor vulnerabilities continuously
   + ISO/IEC 27001: calls for risk assessment and treatment plans

- PCI DSS: mandates regular scans and remediation of cardholder environments

Strategic Importance

Effective vulnerability management:

- Reduces potential for exploit by threat actors
- Enhances visibility across assets and risks
- Strengthens compliance posture
- Facilitates operational coordination between security and IT teams
- Enables informed decision-making through measurable metrics

Key terminology and lifecycle stages

Key Terminology

Understanding these terms creates clarity across teams and strengthens alignment with compliance frameworks:

Term	Definition
Vulnerability	A flaw or weakness in a system that can be exploited to compromise security.
Threat	A potential cause of an unwanted incident, which may result in harm.
Exploit	A method or tool used to take advantage of a vulnerability.

Exposure	A state in which a vulnerability is accessible to a threat actor.
Risk	The potential impact and likelihood of a threat exploiting a vulnerability.
Remediation	Actions taken to fix or eliminate the vulnerability (e.g., applying patches).
Mitigation	Steps taken to reduce the impact or likelihood of a vulnerability being exploited.
Compensating Controls	Alternative measures that reduce risk when standard remediation isn't feasible.
False Positive	A reported vulnerability that doesn't actually exist.
CVSS (Common Vulnerability Scoring System)	A standardized way to assess the severity of vulnerabilities.
ZeroDay	A vulnerability that is exploited before the vendor becomes aware or issues a fix.
Patch Management	The process of distributing and applying updates to software components.

Vulnerability Management Lifecycle Stages

This lifecycle is iterative, structured, and essential to maintaining security posture:

1. Asset Discovery & Classification

- Identify all hardware, software, cloud, and endpoint assets.

- Group assets by business function and criticality.

2. Vulnerability Detection

- Use scanners like Nessus, Qualys, or Rapid7 to identify vulnerabilities.
- Scan types include:
- Unauthenticated scans: Surface-level assessments
- Authenticated scans: Deeper analysis with credentials
- Results are mapped to CVEs and CVSS scores.

3. Vulnerability Assessment

- Prioritize findings based on:
- CVSS score
- Exploit availability
- Business impact
- Asset exposure and criticality
- Assess false positives and context-based relevance.

4. Remediation Planning

- Coordinate with IT and DevOps teams for patch deployment or configuration updates.
- Identify any compensating controls or temporary workarounds.
- Schedule maintenance windows, QA testing, or rollout plans.

5. Remediation Execution

- Apply patches or reconfigure systems.
- Decommission vulnerable assets if necessary.
- Validate fixes through rescan or manual verification.

6. Reporting & Metrics

- Track metrics like:
- Mean time to remediate (MTTR)
- Total vulnerabilities discovered/resolved
- Percentage by severity level
- Generate dashboards for executives and audit readiness.

7. Review & Improvement

- Analyze trends and lessons learned.
- Refine scanning schedules, assessment criteria, and remediation procedures.
- Adjust policies to align with evolving threat landscapes and compliance requirements.
- Integrations with Broader Cybersecurity Frameworks
- Vulnerability management aligns with key standards:
- NIST CSF: PR.IP12, DE.CM8, RS.MI3
- ISO/IEC 27001: A.12.6.1, A.12.6.2
- CIS Controls v8: Control 07 (Continuous Vulnerability Management)

- FISMA: Continuous Monitoring requirements

The Role of Vulnerability Management in Cybersecurity Programs

Vulnerability management plays a pivotal role in the strategic and operational effectiveness of cybersecurity programs. It is the bridge between knowing what is weak and ensuring it does not stay that way. Here's how it functions within the broader security ecosystem:

Core Role in Cybersecurity Programs

Vulnerability management supports cybersecurity programs by helping to:

1. **Proactively Reduce Attack Surface**
    - Identifies exploitable weaknesses before threat actors can capitalize on them.
    - Supports defensive layers (firewalls, IDS/IPS, endpoint security) by ensuring fewer gaps exist in the underlying systems.
2. **Enable Risk-Based Decision Making**
    - Transforms raw scan data into prioritized actions based on business impact and exploitability.
    - Helps CISOs and risk officers balance remediation efforts with operational needs using CVSS scores and asset criticality.
3. **Support Regulatory Compliance**

- Ensures continuous monitoring and vulnerability identification required by frameworks like NIST, ISO 27001, FISMA, and PCI DSS.
- Generates auditable evidence of vulnerability management activities, exceptions, and remediation timelines.

4. **Facilitate Incident Prevention and Response**
    - Reduces the number of potential entry points for attackers, especially those used in real-world breaches (e.g., Log4Shell).
    - Enhances incident response readiness by mapping vulnerabilities to potential attack vectors.
5. **Promote Cyber Hygiene and Resilience**
    - Encourages consistent patching and secure configuration practices across the organization.
    - Limits the exposure window for newly discovered threats—particularly zero-day vulnerabilities.

Integration Points with Other Cybersecurity Functions

Function	Connection to Vulnerability Management
Asset Management	Accurate inventories are essential for knowing where to scan and prioritize.
Threat Intelligence	Helps correlate vulnerabilities with current exploits in the wild.
Patch Management	Executes remediation plans identified through vulnerability scans.

Security Operations Center (SOC)	Uses vulnerability data for real-time correlation with SIEM alerts.
Compliance & Audit	Relies on scan reports, remediation metrics, and policy adherence.
Risk Management	Leverages vulnerability data to quantify and mitigate technical risks.

Value to Cybersecurity Maturity

Vulnerability management contributes to advancing an organization's maturity by:

- Automating security tasks, enabling scale and consistency
- Improving metrics and visibility, such as MTTR and remediation rates
- Aligning security with business priorities, reducing friction between teams
- Building a defensible security posture, both for operations and audits

Strategic Takeaway

Think of vulnerability management as a foundational layer. While other security domains—like identity, endpoint protection, or network monitoring—focus on specific threats and technologies, vulnerability management ensures that the entire ecosystem is fortified and adaptable.

Chapter Three

Risk-Based Prioritization

Understanding Risk vs. Severity

Distinguishing between risk and severity is central to prioritizing vulnerabilities effectively in a cybersecurity program. While they are often discussed together, they serve distinct analytical purposes:

Understanding Severity

Severity refers to the technical impact a vulnerability could have if exploited, often measured in isolation from context.

Key Traits:

- Based on characteristics of the vulnerability itself.
- Commonly scored using the CVSS (Common Vulnerability Scoring System):
- Base score: Evaluates exploitability and impact
- Temporal score: Considers availability of exploit code or fixes
- Environmental score: Reflects asset-specific conditions

Examples:

- A remote code execution flaw in a web server may have a high severity.
- A misconfiguration allowing weak encryption might be medium severity, depending on usage.

Understanding Risk

Risk is a contextual evaluation that considers the likelihood of exploitation and the impact on your specific environment.

Key Components:

- Threat likelihood: Are attackers actively exploiting this?
- Asset value: How critical is the affected system to business operations?
- Exposure: Is the system internet-facing or internally segmented?
- Existing controls: Are there firewalls, IDS, or compensating safeguards in place?

Risk ≠ Severity

A vulnerability with high severity may pose low risk if the asset is isolated and well-protected. Conversely, a medium-severity flaw could present high risk if it affects a sensitive system with poor safeguards.

Risk vs. Severity in Prioritization

Scenario	Severity	Risk	Action
SQL injection on a public-facing login page	High	High	Immediate remediation
Outdated software on isolated test server	High	Low	Schedule for future patch cycle
Misconfigured S3 bucket hosting sensitive data	Medium	High	Urgent reconfiguration
Unused port open on development environment	Low	Low	Document and monitor

Strategic Integration

Effective vulnerability management programs use risk-based prioritization to allocate remediation resources. This prevents "patch everything" overload and ensures meaningful security improvements.

CVSS Scoring and Business Impact Analysis

Understanding CVSS scoring and Business Impact Analysis (BIA) is essential for translating technical vulnerabilities into strategic risk decisions. These concepts complement each other within vulnerability management.

CVSS (Common Vulnerability Scoring System)

CVSS provides a standardized way to evaluate the severity of a vulnerability. It is widely used to objectively quantify technical impact and guide prioritization.

CVSS Structure

CVSS consists of three metric groups:

Metric Group	Description
Base Score	Intrinsic characteristics of a vulnerability (e.g., exploitability, impact)
Temporal Score	Factors that change over time (e.g., availability of exploit code or remediation)
Environmental Score	Contextual factors in your organization (e.g., asset importance, exposure level)

Score Range: 0.0 (None) → 10.0 (Critical)

Severity Ratings:

- – None
- 0.1–3.9 – Low
- 4.0–6.9 – Medium
- 7.0–8.9 – High
- 9.0–10.0 – Critical

Base Metrics Breakdown:

- Attack Vector (AV) – Local, Adjacent, Network
- Attack Complexity (AC) – Low, High
- Privileges Required (PR) – None, Low, High
- User Interaction (UI) – Required/Not Required

- Confidentiality/Integrity/Availability Impact – None, Low, High
- Tools like NVD, Nessus, Qualys, and CVSS calculators automate the scoring and allow customization for environmental factors.

Business Impact Analysis (BIA)

BIA assesses the potential consequences to operations if a vulnerability were exploited—not just its technical severity.

Purpose:

- Identifies critical business processes and assets
- Estimates financial, operational, reputational, and legal impacts
- Supports risk-based prioritization by combining CVSS scores with business context

Key BIA Elements:

Element	Description
Asset Criticality	How essential the affected asset is to business continuity
Data Sensitivity	The type of data exposed (e.g., PII, financials, healthcare records)
Process Dependency	Whether vulnerable assets support key operations or systems

Downtime Tolerance	Acceptable outage duration before impact becomes significant
Regulatory Exposure	Risk of noncompliance or breach of regulatory mandates
Revenue or Reputation Impact	Potential loss in customer trust, market value, or profit

CVSS vs. BIA: Why You Need Both

Aspect	**CVSS Scoring**	**Business Impact Analysis**
Focus	Technical vulnerability impact	Organizational and operational consequences
Scope	Asset agnostic	Asset and process specific
Used By	Security teams	Business leaders, risk managers, and auditors
Benefit	Objective severity rating	Strategic prioritization and justification

Combined Application Example

Imagine two vulnerabilities:

1. CVSS 9.8 – on a nonproduction system with no sensitive data.
2. CVSS 6.5 – on a financial database handling payroll.

Despite the lower CVSS, the second may warrant a higher priority due to greater business impact.

Aligning Priorities with Organizational Risk Appetite

Aligning vulnerability management priorities with an organization's risk appetite ensures that resources are directed where they matter most and that security measures support—not hinder—business goals.

What Is Risk Appetite?

Risk appetite is the amount and type of risk an organization is willing to accept in pursuit of its objectives. It is shaped by business strategy, regulatory obligations, stakeholder expectations, and operational resilience.

Key Attributes:

- Expressed in qualitative (e.g., conservative, moderate, aggressive) or quantitative terms
- Can differ by business unit, asset type, or threat category
- Documented in enterprise risk frameworks and governance policies

How Vulnerability Management Aligns with Risk Appetite

1. **Risk-Based Prioritization**
    - Use CVSS scores in combination with Business Impact Analysis (BIA) to assign priority levels.
    - Example: A critical CVSS score on a test server may be deprioritized if the business deems it low risk.

2. **Tailored Remediation Policies**
   - High risk tolerance: Focus on rapid remediation of only critical and high-risk findings.
   - Low risk tolerance: Address a broader set of vulnerabilities, including medium and low severity.
3. **Governance Integration**
   - Sync vulnerability policies with enterprise risk frameworks such as:
   - NIST Risk Management Framework (RMF)
   - ISO 31000 Risk Management
   - COSO ERM Framework
   - Align reporting metrics with governance dashboards used by risk committees and boards.
4. **Exception and Acceptance Protocols**
   - Define formal risk acceptance processes for non-remediated vulnerabilities (with documented justification).
   - Support compensating controls where immediate remediation conflicts with business operations.
5. **Asset Categorization**
   - Map criticality of assets to organizational risk appetite.
   - Example: Customer-facing systems may have zero tolerance for vulnerabilities; internal systems may tolerate delay.

6. **Board-Level Communication**

    - Translate technical findings into business-relevant insights using risk language.
    - Present vulnerability trends and exceptions in terms of potential financial, reputational, or operational impact.

Strategic Outcome

When vulnerability management reflects an organization's risk appetite, it:

- Prevents over-engineering controls that disrupt productivity
- Avoids under-protecting key business functions
- Enhances stakeholder confidence by demonstrating a risk-aware security posture.

Chapter Four

Vulnerability Assessment Tools

Overview Of Leading Tools: Nessus, Qualys, Rapid7 Insight vm, Splunk

Here's a comprehensive overview of four leading tools in vulnerability management and security analytics, designed to help IT cybersecurity specialists select, integrate, and optimize these technologies in enterprise environments:

1. Nessus by Tenable

Type: Vulnerability Scanner

Focus: Network-based scanning for known vulnerabilities

Key Features:

- Detects software flaws, misconfigurations, missing patches, and compliance violations
- Supports CVE/CVSS integration and custom scan templates
- Offers both authenticated and unauthenticated scanning

- Lightweight and highly configurable
- Often used for internal network, system, and infrastructure assessments

Use Cases:

- Scanning Windows/Linux servers for patch gaps
- Running credentialed scans on workstations
- Detecting default configurations on routers and firewalls

2. Qualys VMDR (Vulnerability Management Detection and Response)

Type: Cloud-native Vulnerability Management Suite

Focus: Continuous scanning, asset discovery, and risk-based remediation

Key Features:

- Cloud agent for real-time vulnerability monitoring across diverse assets
- Integrates asset discovery, vulnerability detection, threat intelligence, and patching
- Provides detailed remediation guidance and automation workflows
- Strong support for hybrid environments (on-prem, cloud, container)

Use Cases:

- Monitoring remote endpoints and cloud workloads with agents
- Aligning vulnerability data with PCI DSS or ISO 27001 compliance efforts
- Automating patch deployment via integrated Qualys Patch Management

3. Rapid7 Insight VM

Type: Cloud-based Vulnerability Management Platform

Focus: Visibility, prioritization, and remediation automation

Key Features:

- Live dashboards with asset group segmentation and risk scoring
- Remediation workflows with ticketing system integration (e.g., Jira, ServiceNow)
- Leverages Real Risk score—a proprietary metric combining CVSS, asset exposure, and threat intelligence
- Strong API support for orchestration with SIEM and SOAR platforms

Use Cases:

- Prioritizing vulnerabilities with exploit availability data (Metasploit integration)
- Coordinating remediation with IT operations

- Customizing risk scoring based on asset criticality and environmental context

4. Splunk (with Splunk enterprise security)

Type: Security Information and Event Management (SIEM)

Focus: Log analysis, security monitoring, and threat detection

Key Features:

- Aggregates logs from vulnerability scanners, endpoints, firewalls, cloud services, and applications
- Correlates vulnerability findings with real-time security events
- Dashboards and alerts for SOC analysts, auditors, and leadership
- Integrates with vulnerability management tools via add-ons and connectors

Use Cases:

- Monitoring for exploit attempts following a known CVE
- Validating remediation success via log correlation
- Supporting compliance reporting (HIPAA, FISMA, NIST)

Choosing the Right Tool

Tool	Best For	Deployment
Nessus	Lightweight scanning and config audits	Agentless or scanner-based

Qualys VMDR	Full spectrum VM + patch automation	Cloud agent model
Rapid7 InsightVM	Risk-based prioritization and remediation	Agent + web-based dashboard
Splunk	Threat correlation and SIEM integration	On-prem or cloud-based

Tool Selection Criteria

Selecting the right security and vulnerability management tools—like Nessus, Qualys, InsightVM, or Splunk—depends on your organization's environment, goals, and resources. Here's a detailed breakdown to guide evaluation and selection:

Key Tool Selection Criteria

1. **Functional Coverage**
    - Core Capabilities: Does the tool support vulnerability scanning, asset inventory, patch management, and threat prioritization?
    - Compliance Alignment: Is it compatible with standards like FISMA, ISO 27001, NIST, and PCI DSS?
    - Extended Features: Correlation with threat intelligence, ticketing system integration, or SIEM workflows.
2. **Scalability & Deployment Model**
    - Environment Fit: Agent-based vs. agentless? Cloud-native vs. on-premise?
    - Asset Coverage: Can it manage endpoints, containers, mobile devices, and cloud workloads?

- Multitenancy: Useful for MSSPs or distributed organizational structures.

3. **Security & Privacy**
    - Data Encryption: Are scan results and communications encrypted in transit and at rest?
    - Role-Based Access Control: Supports least privilege principles?
    - Data Residency Controls: Particularly important for organizations with regional compliance obligations.
4. **Cost and Licensing Model**
    - Pricing Structure: Subscription-based, asset-based, usage-based?
    - Hidden Costs: Add-ons for dashboards, integrations, or extended support?
    - Return on Investment: Time value and operational efficiencies.
5. **Reporting and Dashboards**
    - Visualization Tools: Are results easy to digest for both technical and executive audiences?
    - Custom Report Support: Does it allow tailored reporting per business unit or compliance domain?
    - Automated Alerts: Real-time, scheduled, or event-triggered notifications?

6. **Integration & API Support**
   - SIEM Compatibility: Easy integration with Splunk, QRadar, LogRhythm, etc.
   - Workflow Automation: Support for orchestration platforms (e.g., ServiceNow, Jira, SOAR tools)
   - RESTful API: Enables custom automation and scripting
7. **Ease of Use**
   - User Experience: Intuitive UI? Role-based dashboards?
   - Learning Curve: Does it require niche expertise or training?
   - Documentation & Support: Accessible knowledge base and responsive vendor support?

Example: Mapping Tools to Criteria

Criteria	Nessus	Qualys VMDR	InsightVM	Splunk ES
Functional Depth	Strong scanning	End-to-end VM + Patch	Risk scoring + tickets	SIEM and correlation
Deployment Model	Scanner-based	Cloud agent model	Cloud dashboard + agent	On-prem or cloud
Reporting & Visualization	Basic	Rich dashboards	Real-time dashboards	Advanced
Integration	Limited API	API + patching	SIEM, ticketing, SOAR	Broad SIEM ecosystem

Ease of Use	Moderate setup	Turnkey cloud setup	Role-based dashboards	Requires admin training

Deployment and Integration with SIEM and CMDB

Here's a detailed breakdown of how vulnerability management and security tools—like Nessus, Qualys, Rapid7 InsightVM, and Splunk—can be deployed and integrated with SIEM (Security Information and Event Management) and CMDB (Configuration Management Database) systems to enhance visibility, automation, and incident response:

Deployment Models

1. **Nessus**
    - Deployment: Agentless scanner installed on-prem or in cloud environments
    - Integration: Exports scan results via XML, CSV, or API for ingestion into SIEMs like Splunk or QRadar
    - CMDB Linkage: Can enrich CMDBs with vulnerability data via custom scripts or third-party connectors

2. **Qualys VMDR**
    - Deployment: Cloud-native with lightweight agents on endpoints
    - Integration: Built-in connectors for Splunk, ServiceNow, and other SIEMs
    - CMDB Linkage: Syncs asset and vulnerability data with ServiceNow CMDB using native apps

3. **Rapid7 InsightVM**

- Deployment: Cloud-hosted dashboard with optional agents
- Integration: RESTful API and prebuilt integrations with SIEMs (Splunk, LogRhythm) and ITSM platforms
- CMDB Linkage: Can push asset and risk data into CMDBs like ServiceNow via Insight Connect workflows

4. **Splunk Enterprise Security**

- Deployment: On-prem, cloud, or hybrid
- Integration Hub: Acts as the SIEM itself, ingesting logs from scanners, CMDBs, firewalls, and endpoints
- CMDB Linkage: Uses add-ons to pull asset metadata from CMDBs for context-aware alerting

Integration with SIEM

Benefits:

- Centralized Threat Detection: Correlate vulnerability data with network activity and user behavior
- Automated Alerting: Trigger alerts based on exploit attempts tied to known CVEs
- Incident Enrichment: Add asset criticality and patch status to SIEM events for faster triage

Integration Methods:

- Syslog Forwarding: Tools like Nessus and Qualys can send scan logs directly to SIEM

- API Connectors: Rapid7 and Qualys offer native integrations with Splunk and other SIEMs
- Custom Parsers: Splunk can ingest and normalize data from scanners using TA (Technology Add-ons)

Integration with CMDB

Benefits:

- Asset Contextualization: Link vulnerabilities to specific devices, owners, and configurations
- Change Management: Track remediation actions and configuration drift
- Compliance Reporting: Map vulnerabilities to regulatory controls (e.g., NIST, ISO)

Integration Methods:

- Outbound Sync: Tools push asset and vulnerability data to CMDB (e.g., ServiceNow, Device42)
- Inbound Sync: CMDB feeds asset metadata into scanners for targeted assessments
- Bidirectional APIs: Forti SIEM and ServiceNow support two-way sync for incidents and asset updates

Example: Forti SIEM Integration

Forti SIEM offers native support for:

CMDB Sync: Automatically populates or updates external CMDBs like ServiceNow

SIEM Functions: Correlates vulnerability data with behavioral analytics and threat intelligence

SOAR Automation: Triggers playbooks based on CMDB asset status and SIEM alerts

Chapter Five

Asset Discovery and Inventory

The Importance of Accurate Asset Inventories

Accurate asset inventories form the backbone of cybersecurity, IT governance, and operational efficiency. Without a reliable record of all assets, organizations struggle to manage risks, comply with regulations, and plan strategically.

Why They Matter

1. **Cybersecurity Risk Management**
    - Identifies outdated or vulnerable systems.
    - Supports patching and configuration control.
    - Detects unauthorized or rogue devices on the network.
2. **Regulatory Compliance**
    - Required by frameworks such as FISMA, NIST, ISO 27001, HIPAA, and GDPR.
    - Demonstrates control over sensitive data and access points.
    - Provides documentation for audits and compliance checks.

3. **Incident Response & Containment**
    - Speeds up identification of affected assets during a breach.
    - Provides context for asset dependencies and criticality.
    - Enables targeted containment and recovery strategies.
4. **Cost Optimization & Lifecycle Management**
    - Highlights underutilized or redundant assets.
    - Prevents unnecessary purchases and license renewals.
    - Informs budgeting for upgrades and replacements.
5. **Strategic Planning & Decision-Making**
    - Guides technology investments and infrastructure scaling.
    - Aligns IT resources with business objectives.
    - Improves vendor and contract management.
6. **Operational Efficiency**
    - Improves troubleshooting and service desk response times.
    - Streamlines software updates and hardware maintenance.
    - Reduces downtime through greater visibility and control.

Common Challenges

Despite their importance, maintaining accurate inventories is not without difficulties:

- **Shadow IT and BYOD** often introduce hidden assets.
- **Manual tracking** leads to errors and outdated records.

- **Disconnected systems** create data silos.
- **Resource constraints** prevent frequent updates.

Best Practices for Accuracy

To ensure inventories remain reliable:

- Leverage **automated discovery tools** integrated with CMDBs.
- Perform **regular audits** and reconcile findings with physical assets.
- Use **barcodes or RFID tags** for consistent tracking.
- Assign **clear ownership and accountability** for updates.
- Integrate asset management with **ITSM and procurement platforms.**

Passive vs. Active Discovery Methods

Accurate inventories depend on how assets are discovered. Two primary methods—active and passive discovery—offer different benefits.

Active Discovery

Definition: Actively scans the network by sending probes (e.g., pings, SNMP queries, port scans) to identify devices and configurations.

Advantages:

- Real-time visibility into assets.
- Deep inspection of configurations, OS versions, open ports, and vulnerabilities.
- Suitable for compliance audits and penetration testing.

- Can detect inactive or silent assets if scheduled correctly.

Limitations:

- Potentially disruptive for sensitive or legacy systems.
- Requires credentialed access for deeper scans.
- May trigger IDS alerts or false positives.
- Needs careful scheduling to avoid congestion.

Passive Discovery

Definition: Monitors existing traffic (e.g., syslogs, NetFlow, SNMP traps) without sending probes.

Advantages:

- Non-intrusive and safe for high-availability environments.
- Enables continuous monitoring without network impact.
- Detects shadow IT and rogue devices through traffic patterns.
- Useful for legacy systems or segmented networks.

Limitations:

- Cannot detect silent or offline assets.
- Provides limited detail on configurations or vulnerabilities.
- Relies on log aggregation and visibility.
- Less effective for initial asset discovery.

Use Case Comparison

Criteria	Active Discovery	Passive Discovery
Visibility Scope	Deep, targeted	Broad, continuous
Network Impact	Moderate to high	Minimal
Asset Coverage	All reachable assets	Only active assets
Ideal For	Audits, scans, compliance	Monitoring, detecting shadow IT
Examples	Nessus, Qualys, InsightVM	Splunk, NetFlow, SNMP traps

Best Practice: Combine Both

Most mature organizations adopt a **hybrid approach** to asset discovery:

- **Active discovery** provides scheduled deep scans and vulnerability assessments.
- **Passive discovery** offers continuous monitoring and anomaly detection.

Together, they deliver comprehensive visibility, minimize blind spots, and strengthen both security operations and CMDB accuracy.

Integrating Asset Data with Scan Strategies

Effective vulnerability management depends on aligning **asset data with scan strategies.** This integration ensures scans are targeted, efficient, and context-aware, supporting frameworks such as **NIST, FISMA, and ISO 27001.**

Why Integration Matters

- Improves scan accuracy by matching scans to verified asset records.
- Reduces blind spots by ensuring critical assets are never overlooked.
- Prioritizes remediation using asset metadata (business impact, owner, location).
- Demonstrates compliance by mapping scans to regulated asset groups.

Integration Workflow

1. **Asset Inventory Foundation**
    - Source asset data from CMDBs (e.g., ServiceNow, Device42) or discovery tools (Qualys, InsightVM).
    - Include metadata: OS, IP, hostname, business unit, criticality, and owner.
2. **Scan Strategy Alignment**
    - Define scan types (authenticated, unauthenticated, internal, external).
    - Adjust frequency based on risk (e.g., daily for internet-facing assets, monthly for low-risk systems).
    - Group assets by environment (production, development, cloud, on-prem).
3. **Dynamic Targeting**
    - Use tags or labels to auto-assign assets to scan templates.

- Sync scan schedules with CMDB updates.
- Exclude non-scannable or sensitive systems with tailored filters.

4. **Risk-Based Prioritization**
   - Combine vulnerability findings with asset context to calculate risk scores.
   - Prioritize remediation by asset criticality and exploitability.
   - Feed results into SIEM platforms (e.g., Splunk) for correlation with threat activity.

Example: ServiceNow + Qualys Integration

Component	**Functionality**
CMDB (ServiceNow)	Stores asset metadata and relationships
Qualys VMDR	Performs vulnerability scans
Integration App	Syncs asset records and scan results
Workflow Automation	Creates tickets for high-risk vulnerabilities

This setup delivers real-time visibility, automated remediation, and audit-ready reporting.

Best Practices

- Normalize asset data before integration to prevent mismatches.
- Use APIs for **bidirectional synchronization** between scanners and CMDBs.
- Enrich scan results by tagging assets with business context.

- Perform regular audits to validate alignment of assets and scans.

NIST-Aligned Vulnerability Scan Strategy (Hybrid Cloud)

Environment: Hybrid Cloud (On-prem + Public Cloud)

Framework Reference: NIST Cybersecurity Framework (CSF) & SP 800-53 Rev. 5

1. Identify (ID) – Asset Management & Risk Context

- Maintain a centralized CMDB with metadata (location, owner, criticality).
- Use both passive discovery (NetFlow, Splunk) and active scanning (Qualys, InsightVM).
- Tag cloud workloads with business labels (e.g., "High Availability," "PII").
- Sync with AWS Config, Azure Resource Graph for cloud-native assets.
- Conduct risk assessments (CVSS, exploitability, exposure) to prioritize frequency.

2. Protect (PR) – Configuration & Access Control

- Schedule scans based on classification (e.g., daily for internet-facing, monthly for internal).
- Use authenticated scans for deeper visibility.
- Integrate with patch management tools (WSUS, SCCM, Qualys Patch).

- Restrict scan credentials using least-privilege principles and log all usage.

3. Detect (DE) – Continuous Monitoring

- Feed results into SIEM (Splunk ES, QRadar).
- Correlate vulnerabilities with live threat events (exploit attempts, lateral movement).
- Monitor dashboards for coverage and remediation status.

4. Respond (RS) – Incident Handling & Remediation

- Automate ticket creation for high-risk findings (ServiceNow, Jira).
- Prioritize remediation by combining asset criticality with threat intelligence.
- Document scan results in incident reports and RCA workflows.

5. Recover (RC) – Lessons Learned & Resilience

- Review scan coverage after incidents.
- Update templates and asset groups with new insights.
- Validate fixes through follow-up scans and SIEM correlation.

Hybrid Cloud Integration Map

Component	Tool/Method	Purpose
CMDB	ServiceNow, API sync	Asset inventory & tagging
Vulnerability Scanner	Qualys, InsightVM, Nessus	Active scanning

Passive Discovery	Splunk, NetFlow, SNMP traps	Shadow IT and rogue asset detection
SIEM	Splunk ES, QRadar	Correlation & alerting
Cloud Inventory	AWS Config, Azure Resource Graph	Cloud asset visibility
Ticketing System	ServiceNow, Jira	Remediation workflow automation

Chapter Six

Scan Strategy and Scheduling

Choosing Scan Types: Authenticated vs. Unauthenticated

Selecting between **authenticated** and **unauthenticated** scans is a strategic decision that shapes visibility, risk prioritization, and compliance outcomes.

Authenticated Scans (Credentialed)

Definition:

Performed using valid credentials to log into target systems, simulating the perspective of a trusted user.

Advantages

- Provides deep visibility into system internals (patch levels, configurations, installed software).
- Reduces false positives through direct access to system data.
- Detects privilege escalation paths and misconfigured access controls.

- Aligns with compliance standards such as PCI DSS, HIPAA, and NIST SP 800-53.

Considerations

- Requires careful credential management and secure storage.
- May affect system performance if not properly configured.
- Needs role-based access to limit overexposure.
- Must be authorized and documented for audits.

Unauthenticated Scans (Non-Credentialed)

Definition:

Performed without credentials, simulating an external attacker's perspective.

Advantages

- Quick setup with minimal configuration.
- Safe for perimeter testing and external exposure assessments.
- Identifies public-facing vulnerabilities such as open ports and outdated services.
- Useful for initial reconnaissance and detecting shadow IT.

Considerations

- Limited to surface-level vulnerabilities.
- Cannot detect internal misconfigurations or privilege issues.
- May produce false positives due to lack of system context.

When to Use Each

Use Case	Recommended Scan Type
Internal systems & compliance audits	Authenticated
External perimeter & public assets	Unauthenticated
Privilege escalation testing	Authenticated
Quick security overview	Unauthenticated
Web application logic flaws	Authenticated (with session replay)

Best Practice: Combine Both

The most effective strategy is a **hybrid approach**:

- Use **unauthenticated scans** to simulate external threats.
- Use **authenticated scans** for in-depth internal assessments and compliance validation.
- Compare results to reveal blind spots and validate findings.

Scheduling Scans for Coverage and Minimal Disruption

Scheduling vulnerability scans requires balancing **security visibility** with **operational continuity**. Poor scheduling can cause downtime, bandwidth issues, or user frustration.

Key Principles for Scan Scheduling

1. **Coverage Goals**
    - Scan all critical assets regularly (servers, endpoints, cloud workloads).

- Match scan frequency to asset risk and business impact.
- Include newly onboarded assets via CMDB synchronization or dynamic groups.

2. **Disruption Minimization**
   - Run scans during off-peak hours (nights, weekends, or lunch breaks).
   - Avoid overlap with backups, patch windows, or maintenance periods.
   - Notify stakeholders in advance to prevent false alarms and bandwidth strain.

Recommended Scheduling Patterns

Asset Type	Scan Type	Frequency	Timing
Internet-facing servers	Authenticated + External	Daily or every 2 days	Late night or early morning
Internal end-points	Authenticated	Weekly	After business hours
Cloud work-loads	API-based + Agent scans	Daily or contin-uous	Based on cloud ac-tivity
Legacy systems	Passive + Light ac-tive scans	Monthly	Maintenance win-dows
Web applica-tions	Dynamic + Static scans	Weekly or bi-weekly	Off hours or staging env

Tool-Specific Recommendations

Nessus

- Use templates to alternate between exhaustive and lighter scans.
- Schedule scans via the web UI or CLI with cron-like flexibility.
- Prevent overlapping scan windows to reduce job failures.

Qualys VMDR

- Apply dynamic asset tagging to auto-assign scan schedules.
- Use cloud agents for continuous, low-impact scanning.
- Sync scan windows with change management workflows in ServiceNow.

InsightVM

- Schedule scans using **site-level templates** and distributed scan engines.
- Define **maximum scan durations** to prevent overruns.
- Leverage **InsightConnect** to pause or adjust scans during critical operations.

Splunk (SIEM Integration)

- Correlate scan schedules with **event logs** to detect anomalies.
- Configure **alerts** for scan failures or threshold exceedances.
- Integrate with the CMDB to validate scan coverage against asset inventories.

Best Practices for Scan Scheduling

- **Stagger scans** across asset groups to reduce bandwidth strain.
- Exclude **low-risk assets** from frequent scans to conserve resources.
- Use **incremental scanning** where supported to shorten run times.
- Monitor scan performance and adjust schedules as needed.
- Document scan windows in the **vulnerability management policy** for consistency.

Handling Sensitive Systems and Legacy Environments

Securing sensitive and legacy systems requires a balanced approach — protecting critical operations while maintaining compliance and minimizing disruption.

What Are Sensitive and Legacy Systems?

- **Sensitive Systems:** Handle confidential, regulated, or mission-critical data (e.g., financial records, healthcare systems, ICS/SCADA).
- **Legacy Systems:** Outdated platforms (e.g., Windows XP, Server 2003, COBOL apps) that remain in use due to dependencies, cost, or compliance needs.

Risks and Challenges

Risk Area	Impact on Legacy/Sensitive Systems
Lack of Patching	Exposure to known exploits and vulnerabilities.
Tool Incompatibility	Modern EDR/SIEM tools may not support older OS versions.
Operational Fragility	Updates or scans may disrupt mission-critical functions.
Compliance Gaps	Difficulty meeting frameworks (NIST, FISMA, HIPAA, ISO 27001).
Limited Visibility	Weak logging, monitoring, and anomaly detection.

Security Strategies

1. **Isolation & Network Segmentation**
    - Place legacy systems in dedicated VLANs or air-gapped zones.
    - Restrict access via firewalls and ACLs.
    - Apply micro-segmentation to prevent lateral movement.
2. **Agentless Forensic Scanning**
    - Use tools such as **THOR/THOR Thunderstorm** for offline or unsupported systems.
    - Detect malware, anomalies, and backdoors without installing agents.
3. **Virtual Patching & Wrappers**
    - Apply **network-level protections** to block threats before they reach legacy systems.

- Use middleware for encryption, MFA, and intrusion detection.

4. **Access Controls & Monitoring**
   - Enforce least privilege and multifactor authentication.
   - Deploy IDS/IPS and centralized log aggregation (e.g., Splunk) for visibility.
5. **Incident Response Planning**
   - Develop tailored playbooks for legacy environments.
   - Use forensic tools and non-intrusive containment strategies.

Best Practices for Legacy Systems

- Document dependencies and their business impact.
- Audit configurations regularly for drift or unauthorized changes.
- Encrypt sensitive data at rest and in transit (even via external controls).
- Train staff in secure handling of legacy systems.
- Plan phased modernization or containerization where feasible.

Compliance Mapping (NIST SP 800-53)

Control Family	Relevant Controls
System & Communication Protection	SC-7 (Boundary Protection), SC-12 (Cryptography)
Access Control	AC-2 (Account Management), AC-6 (Least Privilege)
Audit & Accountability	AU-2 (Audit Events), AU-6 (Audit Review)
Risk Assessment	RA-3 (Risk Assessment), RA-5 (Vulnerability Scanning)

Legacy System Security Policy (Draft)

Purpose:

Define governance and security controls for legacy systems that remain operational, archived, or pending decommissioning, ensuring sensitive data is protected and compliance with FISMA and ISO 27001 is maintained.

Scope:

Applies to:

- End-of-life operating systems (e.g., Windows XP, Server 2003).
- Unsupported applications.
- Archived databases retained for audit or legal requirements.

Policy Statements

1. **System Isolation & Segmentation**

- Place legacy systems in segmented VLANs or DMZs.
- Restrict access via firewalls/ACLs.
- Disable remote access unless explicitly approved.

2. **Compensating Controls**
   - Apply virtual patching and intrusion prevention where updates aren't possible.
   - Enforce encryption and authentication via middleware/wrappers.
3. **Monitoring & Logging**
   - Forward logs to SIEM platforms (e.g., Splunk).
   - Monitor for anomalous behavior.
   - Retain logs for at least 90 days (or per regulatory requirements).
4. **Access Control**
   - Enforce least privilege and role-based access.
   - Require MFA for admin access.
   - Review access logs quarterly.
5. **Vulnerability Management**
   - Use agentless or passive scans.
   - Document known vulnerabilities and risk acceptance.
   - Reassess risk quarterly or after major changes.
6. **Documentation & Ownership**
   - Maintain inventory with business justification.

- Assign system owners for oversight.
- Include legacy systems in the System Security Plan (SSP).

7. **Incident Response**
   - Integrate legacy systems into IR playbooks.
   - Define non-disruptive containment procedures.
   - Document lessons learned.
8. **Decommissioning Strategy**
   - Define retirement timelines.
   - Securely migrate or sanitize data.
   - Retain audit trails after decommissioning.

Compliance Mapping

Control Area	**FISMA (NIST SP 800-53)**	**ISO/IEC 27001:2022**
Asset Inventory	CM-8	A.5.9, A.8.1
Access Control	AC-2, AC-6	A.9.1, A.9.2
System Isolation	SC-7	A.13.1, A.13.2
Vulnerability Management	RA-5, SI-2	A.12.6.1
Logging & Monitoring	AU-2, AU-6	A.12.4.1, A.12.4.3
Incident Response	IR-4, IR-5	A.16.1
Risk Assessment	RA-3	A.6.1.2, A.6.1.3
Decommissioning	MP-6, SC-12	A.8.3.2, A.11.2.7

Chapter Seven

Vulnerability Classification and Validation

Differentiating False Positives and Actionable Findings

Accurately distinguishing between **false positives** and **actionable findings** is vital in vulnerability management and incident response. Misclassification wastes resources, delays remediation, and increases risk.

Key Definitions

- **False Positive:** A flagged vulnerability or alert that does not pose a real threat.
- **Actionable Finding:** A verified issue that requires remediation to reduce risk or prevent exploitation.

How to Differentiate Them

1. **Contextual Validation**
   - *False Positive:* Flagged by a scanner but rendered non-exploitable by configuration.

- *Example:* A web server flagged for SSLv3 support when SSLv3 is actually disabled.
- *Actionable Finding:* Confirmed exploitable misconfiguration or vulnerability validated through analysis.

2. **Reproducibility**
   - *False Positive:* Cannot be reproduced in testing.
   - *Actionable Finding:* Exploitation succeeds, demonstrating impact (e.g., privilege escalation, data exposure).
3. **Tool Correlation**
   - *False Positive:* Flagged by one tool but not corroborated by others.
   - *Actionable Finding:* Validated across multiple tools (e.g., Nessus + Qualys + manual testing).
4. **Business Impact**
   - *False Positive:* No effect on confidentiality, integrity, or availability.
   - *Actionable Finding:* Directly affects critical assets, compliance, or operations.
5. **Exploitability**
   - *False Positive:* Based on outdated or theoretical exploits.
   - *Actionable Finding:* Exploit available in CVE repositories or actively used by threat actors.

Recommended Practices:

- Apply CVSS plus contextual scoring for prioritization.

- Tag and suppress confirmed false positives in the VM platform.
- Document validation steps for audit and compliance.
- Involve SMEs and system owners for environment-specific input.
- Keep scanner plugins and signatures up to date.

Categorizing Vulnerabilities

Organizing vulnerabilities into categories helps streamline remediation and align with compliance frameworks like FISMA and ISO 27001.

1. Misconfigurations

- **Examples:** Default credentials, open unused ports, missing headers, directory listing enabled, insecure cookie flags.
- **Impact:** Data leakage, unauthorized access, expanded attack surface.
- **Mitigation:** Harden configurations, perform regular audits, apply secure baselines.

2. Outdated Software / Vulnerable Components

- **Examples:** Legacy plugins, unpatched Apache Struts, Log4j, or deprecated APIs.
- **Impact:** Remote code execution, supply chain compromise, compliance violations.
- **Mitigation:** Maintain an SBOM, use SCA tools, apply WAF-based virtual patching.

3. Missing Patches

- **Examples:** OS patches, browser/database updates, firmware upgrades.
- **Impact:** Exploitable CVEs, automated bot attacks, persistent threats.
- **Mitigation:** Automate patch management, prioritize by CVSS/exploitability, validate post-deployment.

4. Social Engineering Vulnerabilities

- **Examples:** Phishing, tailgating, impersonation of IT staff.
- **Impact:** Credential theft, physical access breaches, malware delivery.
- **Mitigation:** Awareness training, physical controls, simulated phishing campaigns.

Severity Mapping:

Category	Severity Range	Notes
Misconfigurations	Low → Medium	Numerous, individually less critical.
Outdated Software	High → Critical	Known exploits, major compliance issues.
Missing Patches	Medium → Critical	Severity depends on CVE and exposure.
Social Engineering	Variable	Depends on compromised access level.

Exploitability Assessment and Threat Intelligence Integration

Exploitability Assessment evaluates the likelihood that a vulnerability can be successfully exploited. It goes beyond CVSS to consider real-world factors.

Key Factors:

- Availability of public or PoC exploits.
- Complexity of exploitation.
- Remote vs. local accessibility.
- Severity of potential impact.
- Evidence of active exploitation in the wild.

Resources:

- CISA Known Exploited Vulnerabilities (KEV).
- Exploit Prediction Scoring System (EPSS).
- Threat intel feeds (Mandiant, Recorded Future).
- Scanners with exploitability tagging (Qualys, InsightVM).

Threat Intelligence Integration

Threat intelligence enriches vulnerability data with **real-world attacker behavior** and evolving trends.

Benefits:

- **Prioritized Remediation:** Focus on vulnerabilities actively exploited.

- **Contextual Risk Scoring:** Combine CVSS with exploitability + business impact.
- **Attack Path Mapping:** Understand vulnerabilities in the context of kill chains.
- **Early Warning:** Identify emerging threats proactively.

Sources:

- Open source intelligence (OSINT, NVD, MITRE ATT&CK).
- Commercial platforms (Palo Alto CTEM, Nucleus VIP).
- Internal telemetry (SIEM, EDR, XDR).
- Dark web monitoring and breach data.

Combined Workflow Example

Step	Action
Discovery	Scan assets for vulnerabilities.
Threat Enrichment	Tag vulnerabilities with exploitability + threat actor activity.
Prioritization	Rank findings by exploitability, asset criticality, and threat relevance.
Validation	Confirm via exploitation simulation or BAS (Breach/Attack Simulation).
Remediation	Patch, isolate, or apply compensating controls.

Feedback Loop	Update threat models, refine prioritization, and improve workflows.

Conducting Effective Exploitability Assessments

An effective exploitability assessment is critical for prioritizing vulnerabilities based on real-world risk, not just theoretical severity. By combining scoring models, threat intelligence, and contextual analysis, organizations can ensure that remediation efforts target vulnerabilities most likely to be exploited.

Core Best Practices for Exploitability Assessment

1. **Establish a Clear Framework**
    - Define goals: focus on likelihood of exploitation rather than volume.
    - Align with standards: use CVSS, EPSS, and recognized threat intelligence feeds.
    - Document methodology for **auditability and repeatability**.
2. **Use Multiple Scoring Models**
    - CVSS (Common Vulnerability Scoring System): baseline severity rating.
    - EPSS (Exploit Prediction Scoring System): probability of exploitation within 30 days.
    - CISA KEV Catalog: confirms vulnerabilities actively exploited in the wild.
3. **Integrate Threat Intelligence**
    - Enrich findings with data from:

- **Open-source feeds** (NVD, MITRE ATT&CK).
- **Commercial platforms** (Recorded Future, Mandiant).
- **Internal telemetry** (SIEM, EDR, XDR).
- Prioritize vulnerabilities that are **actively targeted by threat actors.**

4. **Assess Environmental Context**
   - Evaluate **asset criticality** (e.g., internet-facing vs. internal systems).
   - Consider business impact and regulatory requirements.
   - Map vulnerabilities into **attack paths** or **kill chains.**
5. **Validate Exploitability**
   - Use **breach/attack simulation tools** or controlled manual testing.
   - Confirm exploit success or failure in a **sandbox environment.**
   - Tag findings as *"Confirmed Exploitable," "Theoretical,"* or *"False Positive."*
6. **Automate Where Possible**
   - Deploy scanners with **exploitability tagging** (Qualys, InsightVM).
   - Automate enrichment with threat feeds and scoring models.
   - Use dashboards for **real-time prioritization and reporting.**
7. **Maintain a Feedback Loop**
   - Update exploitability scores as threats evolve.

- Reassess after significant changes (e.g., new exploit discovered, asset role change).
- Share insights with vulnerability management and incident response teams.

Compliance Alignment

Effective exploitability assessments align with key compliance frameworks, including **FISMA (NIST SP 800-53)** and **ISO/IEC 27001:2022**.

Practice	**FISMA (NIST SP 800-53)**	**ISO/IEC 27001:2022**
Threat Intelligence Integration	RA-5, SI-4	A.5.7, A.6.1.3
Exploitability Scoring	RA-3, RA-5	A.6.1.2, A.12.6.1
Asset Contextualization	CM-8, CA-9	A.5.9, A.8.1
Validation & Testing	SI-2, CA-8	A.12.1.1, A.14.2.8

Chapter Eight

Remediation and Exception Handling

Creating Effective Remediation Plans

An effective remediation plan transforms **insight into action** — ensuring vulnerabilities are not just identified but strategically addressed with accountability and compliance.

Core Components of a Remediation Plan

1. **Problem Statement**
    - Clearly define the issue or vulnerability.
    - Include affected systems, assets, and potential impact.
    - Reference detection sources (audit, scan, or incident).
2. **Root Cause Analysis**
    - Identify underlying causes (e.g., misconfiguration, outdated software).
    - Use structured methods such as the **5 Whys** or **Fishbone Diagram.**
    - Document contributing factors (technical, procedural, human).

3. **Risk Assessment**
    - Evaluate severity using CVSS, EPSS, or business impact scoring.
    - Determine likelihood of exploitation and regulatory implications.
    - Prioritize based on asset criticality and threat intelligence.
4. **Remediation Objectives**
    - Define measurable goals (e.g., patch deployment, configuration hardening).
    - Align with compliance standards (e.g., NIST SP 800-53, ISO 27001 A.12.6.1).
    - Include both short-term containment and long-term resolution.
5. **Action Plan**
    - Break tasks into steps with owners, deadlines, and dependencies.
    - Outline technical steps (patching, revoking access, hardening).
    - Specify validation methods (e.g., rescans, configuration reviews).
6. **Resource Allocation**
    - Assign personnel, tools, and budget.
    - Involve SMEs, system owners, and change management.
    - Provide test environments where needed.
7. **Communication Strategy**

- Notify stakeholders and affected users.
- Maintain transparency with regulators if applicable.
- Track and report progress via dashboards.

8. **Monitoring & Validation**
    - Confirm remediation effectiveness with follow-up scans or manual validation.
    - Monitor for recurrence or related risks.
    - Document results and update the risk register.
9. **Documentation & Reporting**
    - Keep **audit-ready records** of all actions.
    - Capture before/after states, logs, and screenshots.
    - Update SSPs, POA&Ms, and compliance documentation.
10. **Continuous Improvement**
    - Feed lessons learned into policy updates and training.
    - Adjust detection and response workflows.
    - Reassess similar systems for systemic weaknesses.

Sample Remediation Plan (Simplified):

Section	Details
Issue	Unpatched Apache vulnerability (CVE-XXXX)
Root Cause	Patch delayed due to change freeze

Risk Level	High (CVSS 9.8, internet-facing asset)
Objective	Apply patch, validate service stability
Tasks	1. Schedule patch window → 2. Apply patch → 3. Retest → 4. Update logs
Owner	Infrastructure Team
Deadline	August 15, 2025
Resources	Patch package, test server, change ticket
Validation	Nessus scan + manual verification
Reporting	Update POA&M, notify CISO, archive logs

Cross-Functional Coordination with IT Operations

Remediation requires **collaboration across IT and business units.** Cross-functional coordination ensures that security efforts align with organizational priorities and do not operate in isolation.

Best Practices for Coordination

1. **Define Shared Goals**
   - Align IT initiatives with business outcomes (uptime, compliance, customer trust).
   - Set measurable OKRs or KPIs that span departments.
2. **Establish Clear Roles & Governance**
   - Use a **RACI matrix** to clarify accountability.
   - Assign cross-department project leads.

3. **Foster Transparent Communication**
   - Hold regular syncs or standups.
   - Use shared platforms (Teams, Jira, Confluence) for visibility.
4. **Integrate Security & Compliance Early**
   - Involve GRC and cybersecurity in planning.
   - Embed NIST, ISO 27001, or CIS controls from the start.
5. **Leverage Collaborative Tools**
   - Use project management systems (Asana, ServiceNow, Trello).
   - Provide dashboards for progress tracking.
6. **Build a Culture of Empathy & Trust**
   - Encourage knowledge sharing and cross-training.
   - Recognize contributions from all departments.
7. **Conduct Joint Risk Assessments**
   - Evaluate risks holistically with IT, security, compliance, and operations.
   - Prioritize based on shared business impact.

Example Use Cases:

Scenario	**Departments Involved**	**Outcome**
Vulnerability Remediation	IT Ops, Security, Compliance	Faster patching with less disruption
Cloud Migration	IT, Finance, Legal, Procurement	Cost-effective and compliant adoption

Incident Response	IT, Security, Legal, Communications	Coordinated containment and messaging
Change Management	IT, HR, Business Units	Smooth rollouts with minimal resistance

Compliance Alignment:

Practice	FISMA (NIST SP 800-53)	ISO/IEC 27001:2022
Governance & Roles	PM-1, CA-6	A.5.1, A.5.3
Communication & Coordination	PL-2, IR-4	A.6.1.1, A.6.1.3
Risk Management	RA-3, RA-5	A.6.1.2, A.8.2
Change Control	CM-3, CM-4	A.12.1.2, A.14.2.9

Managing Exceptions and Documenting Risk Acceptance

Not all risks can be remediated immediately. Mature programs allow for **exception handling** and **formal risk acceptance.**

Key Terms

- **Exception:** Temporary deviation from a policy or control due to business need.
- **Risk Acceptance:** Formal decision to tolerate a known risk without remediation.

Best Practices for Managing Exceptions

1. **Formal Request Process**
    - Standardized forms or GRC platforms.
    - Justification, scope, duration, and compensating controls documented.
2. **Risk Evaluation**
    - Assess likelihood and impact of risk.
    - Classify as low, medium, or high risk.
3. **Approval Workflow**
    - Tiered approvals (system owner → security team → compliance).
    - Executive sign-off for high-risk cases.
4. **Time-Bound Exceptions**
    - Set expiry dates (e.g., 90 days).
    - Require revalidation for renewals.
5. **Monitoring & Review**
    - Maintain a central repository.
    - Conduct periodic reviews to reassess posture.

Documenting Risk Acceptance

1. **Risk Acceptance Statement**
    - Describe risk, impacted systems, and rationale.
    - Include CVSS/EPSS scores and intelligence references.

2. **Stakeholder Sign-Off**
   - Require signatures from system owners, risk owners, and compliance leads.
   - Notify internal audit teams.
3. **Conditions & Compensating Controls**
   - Document residual safeguards (e.g., monitoring, segmentation).
   - Define conditions under which acceptance may be revoked.
4. **Audit-Ready Records**
   - Store in SSPs, POA&Ms, or GRC platforms.
   - Include dates, reviewers, and rationale.

Compliance Mapping:

Practice	**FISMA (NIST SP 800-53)**	**ISO/IEC 27001:2022**
Exception Management	PL-2, RA-5, CA-6	A.5.1, A.6.1.3
Risk Acceptance Documentation	RA-3, RA-7, PM-1	A.6.1.2, A.8.2
Approval & Governance	CA-6, PM-2	A.5.3, A.5.9
Monitoring & Review	SI-4, CA-7	A.12.1.1, A.18.2.3

Chapter Nine

Compliance and Regulatory Alignment

Mapping Findings to Frameworks (NIST SP 800-53, ISO 27001, FISMA)

Mapping vulnerability findings to security frameworks ensures technical issues are translated into **compliance-relevant actions**. This strengthens audit readiness, governance alignment, and overall risk management.

Why Map Findings?

- **Compliance Alignment:** Demonstrates adherence to standards.
- **Audit Readiness:** Simplifies reporting and validation.
- **Risk Prioritization:** Links technical issues to business impact.
- **Control Rationalization:** Avoids duplication across frameworks.

Mapping Strategy

1. **Identify Control Families**
    - Group findings into categories (e.g., access control, patching, configuration).
    - Match to control families:
    - *NIST SP 800-53:* AC (Access Control), CM (Configuration Mgmt), RA (Risk Assessment), SI (System Integrity).
    - *ISO 27001:* Annex A controls (e.g., A.5.15 Least Privilege, A.8.9 Configuration Management).

Use Control Crosswalks

- Leverage mappings such as NIST IR 8477 or SecureFrame guides.
- Use NIST-to-ISO crosswalk tables for consistency.

2. **Align Findings to Control Objectives**
    - Example: *Unpatched critical server*
    - NIST: SI-2 (Flaw Remediation), RA-5 (Vulnerability Scanning).
    - ISO 27001: A.12.6.1 (Technical Vulnerability Management).
    - FISMA: Continuous monitoring and POA&M tracking.
3. **Document in SSPs and POA&Ms**
    - **SSP (System Security Plan):** Map findings to controls.
    - **POA&M (Plan of Action & Milestones):** Track remediation or acceptance.

Sample Mapping Table:

Finding	NIST SP 800-53	ISO/IEC 27001	FISMA Relevance
Unpatched Apache vulnerability	SI-2, RA-5	A.12.6.1	Continuous Monitoring
Default admin credentials	AC-2, AC-6	A.5.15, A.8.2	Identity & Access Controls
Open RDP on public server	SC-7, AC-17	A.5.14, A.8.1	Boundary Protection
Unsupported OS (Win XP)	CM-2, CM-7	A.8.9, A.8.19	Configuration Management

Tips for Effective Mapping:

- Use automated GRC platforms with pre-mapped controls.
- Maintain a **control library** for recurring findings.
- Involve compliance and audit teams early.
- Update mappings as standards evolve (e.g., ISO 27001:2022).

Reporting for Audits and Compliance Assessments

Compliance reporting provides leadership and regulators with **evidence of adherence**, risk posture, and corrective actions.

Core Objectives

- Demonstrate compliance.
- Highlight vulnerabilities and gaps.
- Provide actionable insights for decision-makers.

- Maintain a clear audit trail.

Key Components of an Audit Report

Section	Purpose
Executive Summary	High-level overview of findings and recommendations.
Scope & Objectives	Define systems, controls, or departments reviewed.
Methodology	Describe techniques, tools, and standards applied.
Findings & Observations	Detail control gaps, noncompliance issues, severity.
Corrective Actions	Document remediation steps, owners, and timelines.
Compliance Scorecard	Show KPIs, KRIs, and posture metrics.
Recommendations	Provide governance or strategic improvements.
Appendices	Include evidence, logs, mappings, and reports.

Reporting Best Practices

- Link findings directly to **control IDs** (e.g., NIST AC-2, ISO A.12.6.1).
- Use **dashboards, heat maps, and risk matrices** to visualize posture.
- Maintain version history for audit integrity.
- Tailor content: summaries for executives, details for technical teams.
- Automate reporting with GRC platforms (ServiceNow, Archer, VComply).

Framework-Specific Tips

- **NIST SP 800-53 / FISMA:** Map to control families, document in SSPs and POA&Ms, include continuous monitoring metrics.
- **ISO/IEC 27001:** Reference Annex A controls, update Statement of Applicability, highlight internal audit results.

Sample Finding Entry:

- **Finding:** Unpatched Apache vulnerability on production server.
- **Severity:** High.
- **Framework Mapping:**
- NIST SP 800-53: SI-2, RA-5.
- ISO 27001: A.12.6.1.
- FISMA: Continuous Monitoring.
- **Corrective Action:** Patch deployment scheduled; tracked in POA&M #202504.
- **Owner:** Infrastructure Team.
- **Due Date:** August 15, 2025.

Sample Audit Report Template

1. **Title Page**

- Report Title, Auditor(s), Date, Audit Period.

2. **Executive Summary**
   - Scope, posture, key risks, recommendations.
3. **Scope and Objectives**
   - Systems, processes, or departments reviewed.
4. **Methodology**
   - Audit techniques (interviews, scans, control reviews).
   - Frameworks referenced (NIST 800-53 Rev. 5, ISO 27001:2022).
5. **Findings and Observations**

Finding ID	Description	Severity	Mapped Controls	Evidence
F001	Unpatched Apache vulnerability	High	NIST SI-2, RA-5; ISO A.12.6.1; FISMA CM	Nessus scan #202507
F002	Default admin credentials on server	Medium	NIST AC-2, AC-6; ISO A.5.15; FISMA AC	Config file review
F003	Unsupported OS (Windows XP)	High	NIST CM-2, CM-7; ISO A.8.9; FISMA CM	Asset inventory, logs

6. **Corrective Actions & Recommendations**

Finding ID	Action Plan	Owner	Due Date	Status

F001	Patch via SCCM	Infrastructure	08/15/2025	In Progress
F002	Rotate credentials + MFA enforcement	IAM Team	08/10/2025	Completed
F003	Decommission legacy systems	IT Operations	09/01/2025	Scheduled

7. Compliance Scorecard

Control Family	Reviewed	Compliant	Non-Compliant	Partial
Access Control	12	9	2	1
Configuration Mgmt	8	5	2	1
Vulnerability Mgmt	6	4	2	0

8. Appendices

- Control mapping tables.
- Vulnerability scan reports.
- Interview notes.
- POA&M references.

Demonstrating Continuous Improvement

What Is Continuous Improvement?

Continuous improvement is the **ongoing effort to enhance processes, controls, and outcomes** through incremental changes. It is a core expectation of frameworks such as **ISO 27001, NIST SP 800-53, and FISMA**, which emphasize adaptability, feedback loops, and measurable progress.

Key Elements of Demonstration

1. **Documented Change History**
   - Maintain version-controlled records of policies, controls, and remediation actions.
   - Use SSP revisions, POA&Ms, and audit logs to show progression over time.
2. **Metrics and KPIs**
   - Track vulnerability closure rates, incident response times, and control effectiveness.
   - Use dashboards to visualize trends across reporting cycles.
3. **Feedback Integration**
   - Incorporate lessons learned from audits, incidents, and stakeholder reviews.
   - Demonstrate how feedback directly shaped improvements.
4. **Training and Awareness**
   - Record participation in awareness campaigns and technical training.
   - Highlight increases in completion rates and improved assessment scores.

5. **Control Maturity Assessments**
   - Use models like **NIST CSF tiers** or **CMMI** to show maturity progression.
   - Example: Advancing from "Defined" to "Managed" in vulnerability management.

Sample Evidence Table:

Improvement Area	**Baseline (2024)**	**Current (2025)**	**Evidence**
Patch Compliance Rate	72%	91%	Monthly scan reports, POA&M updates
SSP Review Frequency	Annual	Quarterly	SSP version history, review logs
User Awareness Completion	68%	95%	LMS reports, training dashboards
MFA Coverage	60%	100%	IAM audit logs, policies

Tools to Support Continuous Improvement

- **GRC Platforms:** ServiceNow, Archer, VComply (tracking and reporting).
- **SIEM Dashboards:** Splunk, QRadar (security visualization).
- **Vulnerability Suites:** Nessus, Qualys, Rapid7 (trend analysis).
- **BI Tools:** Power BI, Excel (lightweight dashboards).

Real-World Examples of Continuous Improvement

Technical Enhancements

- Patch Management Optimization: **Moving from quarterly to automated weekly patch cycles.**
- SOAR Implementation: **Automating incident triage and containment, cutting MTTR by 40%.**
- Threat Intel Integration: **Incorporating feeds into SIEM for proactive detection.**

Process Improvements

- Control Maturity Assessments: **Using NIST CSF tiers to benchmark progress.**
- Root Cause Analysis: **Addressing phishing gaps with updated training and email filtering.**
- Policy Refinement: **Enforcing least privilege and MFA after audit findings.**
- Cultural & Organizational Shifts
- Awareness Campaigns: **Gamified phishing simulations to reduce click-through rates.**
- Kaizen Events: **Cross-functional workshops to close workflow gaps (e.g., access revocation).**
- Board Engagement: **Presenting dashboards to executives to align security with business strategy.**

Metrics That Show Progress:

Area	Baseline (2024)	Current (2025)	Evidence
Patch Compliance Rate	72%	91%	Monthly reports, POA&Ms
MFA Coverage	60%	100%	IAM audit logs
Incident Response Time	8 hours	2 hours	SOAR dashboards, IR playbooks
User Awareness Completion	68%	95%	LMS reports, training dashboards

Strategic Foundations for CI

1. **Define an Improvement Vision**
    - Align with organizational goals: risk reduction, audit readiness, and maturity growth.
    - Benchmark using NIST CSF, ISO 27001, or CMMI.
2. **Establish Governance Structures**
    - Create a **Continuous Improvement Committee** or embed CI into existing governance.
    - Assign roles for metric tracking and initiative prioritization.
3. **Integrate CI into Workflows**
    - Add post-remediation reviews and audit retrospectives to identify process gaps.
4. **Leverage Data & Dashboards**

- Track KPIs such as patch compliance and incident response time.
- Visualize performance trends via Splunk or ServiceNow.

5. **Automate Feedback Loops**
   - Trigger POA&M updates when recurring findings are detected.
   - Automate alerts tied to vulnerability or compliance gaps.

Cultural Enablement

6. **Foster a Learning Culture**
   - Run quarterly cyber Kaizen events or "improvement sprints."
   - Encourage cross-functional innovation.
7. **Recognize and Reward**
   - Celebrate achievements (e.g., improved MTTR, audit pass rates).
   - Tie CI participation into performance reviews and recognition.

Sample Implementation Roadmap

Phase	Action	Artifacts/Tools
Initiation	Define CI charter & goals	CI Policy, Governance Charter

Assessment	Establish baselines & maturity	SSPs, Risk Registers
Planning	Prioritize improvement areas	POA&M Tracker, Audit Results
Execution	Implement changes, monitor results	Dashboards, Logs
Review & Sustain	Evaluate outcomes, refine process	RCA Reports, Training Records

Chapter Ten

Metrics, Dashboards, and Reporting

KPIs and Metrics in Cybersecurity

Key **Performance Indicators** (**KPIs**) and **metrics** are essential to measuring progress, aligning security programs with strategic objectives, and demonstrating compliance.

- **KPIs:** High-level indicators tied directly to strategic outcomes.
- **Metrics:** Specific data points that support KPIs. Not every metric is a KPI, but every KPI depends on metrics.

Think of KPIs as the "what" (goals) and metrics as the "how" (measurements).

SMART Framework for KPIs

- **Specific:** Focused on one objective.
- **Measurable:** Supported by quantifiable data.
- **Achievable:** Realistic within available resources.
- **Relevant:** Aligned with organizational goals.
- **Time-Bound:** Monitored within a set timeframe.

Common KPI Categories

Category	Examples
Strategic	Risk reduction %, audit pass rate, control maturity level
Operational	Patch compliance rate, incident response time, scan coverage
Financial	Cost per vulnerability, ROI of tools
Compliance	% controls implemented, POA&M closure rate
User Awareness	Training completion, phishing simulation success

KPIs vs. Metrics

Aspect	KPI	Metric
Purpose	Track achievement of strategic objectives	Monitor operational performance
Scope	High-level, outcome-focused	Detailed, process-focused
Timeframe	Periodic/long-term	Real-time or short-term
Example	"Reduce critical vulnerabilities by 30%"	"Number of critical vulnerabilities found"

Examples in Cybersecurity Context

KPI	Supporting Metrics
Reduce MTTR (Response Time)	Avg. response time, incident volume, automation rate

Improve Patch Compliance	% systems patched, cycle time, missed patch count
Enhance User Awareness	Training completion %, phishing click rate, report rate
Strengthen Access Controls	MFA coverage %, failed login attempts, privilege logs

Tools for Tracking KPIs:

- **SIEM Platforms:** Splunk, QRadar.
- **GRC Tools:** ServiceNow, Archer.
- **Vulnerability Suites:** Nessus, Qualys, Rapid7.
- **Visualization:** Power BI, Tableau.

Sample KPI Dashboard Schema

KPI	Target	Current	Trend	Status
Patch Compliance Rate	95%	91%	↑	On Track
Incident Response Time	<2 hrs	3.5 hrs	↓	Needs Attention
User Awareness Completion	100%	95%	↑	Improving
POA&M Closure Rate	90%	88%	→	Stable

KPI-to-Control Alignment Framework

KPI / Metric	NIST SP 800-53 Control(s)	ISO/IEC 27001 Control(s)	Dashboard Insight

Patch Compliance Rate	SI-2, RA-5	A.12.6.1	Vulnerability closure trends
Incident Response Time	IR-4, IR-5	A.16.1.5	Response readiness, MTTR
MFA Coverage	IA-2	A.9.4.2	Identity assurance
POA&M Closure Rate	CA-5	A.18.2.3	Remediation progress
User Awareness Completion	AT-2	A.7.2.2	Cultural engagement, human risk
Control Effectiveness Score	CA-7	A.6.1.1	Governance and monitoring maturity
Vulnerability Scan Coverage	RA-5	A.12.6.1	Asset visibility, scan completeness
Failed Login Attempts	AC-7	A.9.4.3	Brute force detection, access control

Building Executive-Level Dashboards

Executive dashboards transform technical data into **business-relevant insights** that support strategy, compliance, and decision-making.

Purpose

- Provide **strategic oversight** of risk posture.
- Enable **data-driven decision-making**.
- Ensure **compliance traceability** to frameworks.
- Facilitate **stakeholder communication**.

Core Design Principles

Principle	Description
Clarity	Concise labels, intuitive layouts, minimal clutter.
Relevance	Focus only on KPIs tied to strategic or compliance goals.
Interactivity	Drill-downs into systems, controls, or departments.
Real-Time Data	Connect to SIEM, VM, and GRC platforms for live updates.
Role-Based Views	Tailor dashboards for executives, auditors, and technical teams.

Recommended KPI Categories for Dashboards

- **Vulnerability Management:** Patch rates, scan coverage, critical findings.
- **Incident Response:** MTTR, incident trends, containment rates.
- **Compliance:** % controls implemented, POA&M closures, audit results.
- **Identity & Access:** MFA coverage, failed logins, privilege use.
- **Awareness & Training:** Completion rates, phishing results, reporting levels.

Framework Alignment (Sample)

KPI	NIST SP 800-53	ISO/IEC 27001
Patch Compliance Rate	SI-2, RA-5	A.12.6.1
Incident Response Time	IR-4, IR-5	A.16.1.5
MFA Coverage	IA-2	A.9.4.2
POA&M Closure Rate	CA-5	A.18.2.3
User Awareness Completion	AT-2	A.7.2.2

Tools & Platforms

- **SIEM:** Splunk, QRadar (logs, incident metrics).
- **VM Suites:** Nessus, Qualys, Rapid7 (vulnerability KPIs).
- **GRC:** ServiceNow, Archer, VComply (control and POA&M tracking).
- **Visualization:** Power BI, Tableau (executive reporting).

Sample Executive Dashboard Layout

Executive Cybersecurity Dashboard

1. **Risk Posture Overview**
    - Risk heat map.
    - Top 5 critical vulnerabilities.
2. **Compliance Scorecard**

- % controls implemented (NIST/ISO).
- POA&M closure rate.

3. **Incident Response Metrics**
   - MTTR trends.
   - Open vs. closed incidents.
4. **Identity & Access**
   - MFA coverage.
   - Failed login attempts.
5. **Awareness & Culture**
   - Training completion rates.
   - Phishing simulation results.

Last Updated: [MM/DD/YYYY] | Sources: Splunk, Nessus, ServiceNow

Role-Based Dashboard Strategy

Role	Goals	Data Needs
Executives	Strategic oversight, risk ROI	High-level KPIs, risk heat maps
Auditors	Compliance validation	Control mappings, POA&M status, logs
Technical	Operational performance	Vulnerability and incident details

Views by Role

- **Executive View:** Risk posture, compliance scorecard, top vulnerabilities.
- **Auditor View:** Control traceability, SSP version history, POA&M trackers.
- **Technical View:** Vulnerability dashboards, MTTR, scan coverage.

Tools & Technologies

To support effective metrics, dashboards, and reporting, organizations must leverage a combination of **data aggregation, visualization, automation, and access control tools.**

Function	Recommended Tools
Data Aggregation	Splunk, ServiceNow, Rapid7, Qualys
Visualization	Power BI, Tableau, Grafana
Role-Based Access Control	GRC platforms (Archer, VComply), RBAC modules
Automation & Alerts	SOAR tools, SIEM integrations

Sample Dashboard Layouts

Executive Dashboard

- Risk Heat Map.
- Compliance Scorecard (NIST/ISO aligned).
- POA&M closure rate.
- Top 5 vulnerabilities.

Auditor Dashboard

- Control mapping tables.
- POA&M tracker with due dates.
- SSP revision logs.
- Evidence repository.

Technical Dashboard

- Vulnerability scan coverage.
- Patch compliance trend lines.
- Incident response metrics (MTTR, incident counts).
- System health overview.

Reporting to Technical vs. Business Audiences

Different audiences require **different levels of detail, tone, and structure.** A one-size-fits-all reporting approach often leads to gaps in communication.

Audience Expectations Overview

Aspect	Technical Audience	Business Audience
Focus	Accuracy, detail, system-level insights	Strategic impact, risk posture, ROI
Language	Jargon-friendly, precise, data-heavy	Plain language, concise, outcome-oriented
Format	Tables, logs, diagrams, control IDs	Dashboards, summaries, scorecards

Decision Drivers	Feasibility, control effectiveness	Risk, compliance status, investment priorities
Preferred Evidence	Scan results, logs, control mappings	KPIs, trend charts, executive summaries

Reporting Techniques by Audience

Technical Audience

- **Include:** Vulnerability details, mapped controls (e.g., NIST SI-2, RA-5), system logs, remediation steps.
- **Use:** Structured tables, lifecycle diagrams, flowcharts.
- **Example Report Entry:**
- *Finding:* Unpatched Apache vulnerability.
- *Severity:* High.
- *Mapped Controls:* NIST SI-2; ISO A.12.6.1.
- *Evidence:* Nessus scan #202507.
- *Action:* Patch scheduled via SCCM.

Business Audience

- **Include:** Risk summaries, compliance scores, financial impact, strategic recommendations.
- **Use:** Visual dashboards, heat maps, bullet-point highlights.
- **Example Report Entry:**
- *Risk Summary:* 5 critical vulnerabilities unpatched.

- *Business Impact:* Potential data exposure in customer-facing systems.
- *Compliance Status:* 88% control implementation (ISO/NIST).
- *Recommendation:* Accelerate patch cycle; allocate resources to IAM.

Tips for Effective Dual-Audience Reporting

1. **Layered Structure**
   - Begin with a concise **executive summary** for leadership.
   - Provide drill-downs into technical details for IT/security teams.
2. **Role-Based Views**
   - Use dashboards filtered for executives, auditors, and engineers.
3. **Control Mapping**
   - Always tie findings to **NIST/ISO controls** for traceability.
4. **Avoid Overlap**
   - Keep business reports **outcome-focused** (don't overload with logs).
   - Keep technical reports **evidence-rich** (don't oversimplify findings).

Chapter Eleven

Program Maturity and Continuous Improvement

Assessing Program Maturity with CMMI

The **Capability Maturity Model Integration** (CMMI) is a structured framework to assess and improve organizational processes. For cybersecurity and governance programs, it provides a roadmap to measure current effectiveness and define growth targets.

CMMI Maturity Levels

Level	Name	Description
1	Initial	Ad hoc, reactive, inconsistent processes.
2	Managed	Basic project management processes exist.
3	Defined	Organization-wide standards are documented and followed.
4	Quantitatively Managed	Processes are measured, controlled, and driven by metrics.

5	Optimizing	Focus on innovation and continuous improvement.

Key Process Areas (CMMI v2.0)

- Governance & Implementation Infrastructure.
- Planning & Managing Work.
- Ensuring Quality.
- Managing Business Resilience.
- Delivering & Managing Services.
- Engineering & Developing Products.

How to Assess Maturity

1. **Baseline Assessment** — Internal audits or SCAMPI appraisals.
2. **Gap Identification** — Map current practices to CMMI goals.
3. **Maturity Roadmap** — Prioritize improvements aligned with NIST/ISO frameworks.
4. **Progress Tracking** — Use KPIs (e.g., patch compliance, MTTR, POA&M closure rate).

Integration: CMMI can be paired with **PEMM, ISO 31000,** or **BPMM** for a holistic maturity assessment.

Automation and Orchestration Opportunities

Automation executes tasks. Orchestration coordinates those tasks across workflows — together, they streamline cybersecurity, IT, and compliance operations.

Strategic Opportunities

- **Cybersecurity Operations:**
    - SOAR for incident triage, enrichment, and automated response.
    - Automated vulnerability lifecycle (asset tagging, scan triggers, POA&M generation).
    - Threat intel ingestion and prioritization in SIEM platforms.
- **IT Service Management (ITSM):**
    - Auto-create tickets from scans in ServiceNow/Jira.
    - Orchestrate change management workflows for patching.
    - Automate CMDB updates with cloud/endpoint APIs.
- **Compliance & Governance:**
    - Continuous control monitoring.
    - Automated audit evidence collection.
    - Automated exception workflows for risk acceptance.
- **DevOps & CI/CD:**
    - Embed SAST/DAST scans into pipelines.
    - Use Terraform, Ansible, Kubernetes for secure infrastructure orchestration.
    - Automate rollback/recovery in resilience testing.

Tools & Technologies

Function	Tools
Vulnerability Mgmt	Qualys, Rapid7, Nessus
SOAR	Splunk SOAR, Cortex XSOAR, InsightConnect
ITSM	ServiceNow, Jira, Freshservice
Orchestration Engines	Kubernetes, Terraform, Apache Airflow
Workflow Automation	UiPath, Power Automate, Appian
Threat Intelligence	Mandiant, Recorded Future, CISA KEV

Compliance Mapping:

Opportunity	NIST SP 800-53	ISO/IEC 27001
Automated Patch Deployment	SI-2, CM-6	A.12.6.1
Incident Response Orchestration	IR-4, IR-5	A.16.1.5
Control Monitoring	CA-7, RA-5	A.6.1.3
Audit Evidence Automation	AU-2, AU-6	A.18.1.1

Incorporating Lessons Learned

Post-Incident Reviews

- Conduct root cause analysis (e.g., misconfigured controls, patch delays).
- Measure control effectiveness.
- Update policies, POA&Ms, and playbooks.

Feedback Loops

- Track recurring vulnerability patterns.
- Refine SLA targets and patch prioritization.
- Align feedback across IT, security, and compliance.

Governance Integration

- Map lessons learned directly into updated NIST/ISO control statements.
- Document within audit evidence logs and SSP revisions.

Emerging Trends: AI & Cloud-Native Security

AI-Driven Enhancements

- **Anomaly Detection:** ML models to spot deviations in user/API behavior.
- **Vulnerability Prioritization:** AI risk scoring by exploitability + business impact.
- **Generative AI in SecOps:** Automating triage, threat hunting narratives, and playbooks.

Cloud-Native Scanning

- API-driven scanners for CI/CD pipelines.
- Microservice-aware testing for ephemeral containers.
- Policy-as-Code embedded into IaC templates.

Securing AI Workloads

- Model integrity checks against adversarial manipulation.
- Agentic AI governance to control autonomous decision-making.
- Kubernetes-native frameworks for scalable AI deployments.

CNAI-Aligned Vulnerability Management Strategy

Strategic Pillars

1. Continuous Monitoring — Real-time asset discovery & threat feeds.
2. AI-Augmented Prioritization — ML for exploitability & impact ranking.
3. Cloud-Native Scanning — Integrated into pipelines and workloads.
4. Automated Remediation — Patch/config updates via orchestration.
5. Governance & Feedback — Embed lessons into POA&Ms and audit logs.

Mapping to NIST SP 800-53

CNAI Component	NIST Controls	Purpose
AI-Based Prioritization	RA-5, CA-7, SI-4	Risk scoring, continuous monitoring.
Cloud-Native Scanning	SI-2, CM-8, SA-11	Patch mgmt, asset inventory, secure dev.

Automated Remediation	IR-4, IR-5, CM-6	Incident response & config enforcement.
Feedback Integration	CA-2, PL-2, PM-9	Governance maturity & policy updates.
Threat Intelligence	SI-4(14), AU-6(3)	Threat feeds & log correlation.

Mapping to NIST CSF

CSF Function	CNAI Component	Example Activity
Identify	Asset discovery	CMDB sync + APIs
Protect	Policy-as-Code	IaC templates w/ MFA
Detect	AI anomaly detection	ML-based behavior analytics
Respond	SOAR playbooks	Auto-ticket + containment
Recover	Rollback automation	Backup validation & failover tests

FISMA and ISO 27001 Alignment

- **FISMA (NIST RMF):**
  - Document CNAI practices in SSPs.
  - Generate automated POA&Ms from scan results.
  - Integrate CNAI telemetry into ISCM metrics.
- **ISO/IEC 27001:**
  - AI prioritization aligns with **A.6.1.2, A.12.6.1** (risk & vuln mgmt).

- Cloud-native scanning maps to **A.12.1.2, A.14.2.1** (ops & dev lifecycle).
- Automated remediation supports **A.16.1.5, A.12.4.1** (incident mgmt & logging).
- Threat intelligence links to **A.5.7, A.12.6.1** (threat awareness).

APPENDIX A

Center for Internet Security (CIS): Subject to Modifications Over Time

The **Center for Internet Security (CIS)** publishes the *CIS Critical Security Controls (CIS Controls)*—a prioritized framework of cybersecurity best practices that organizations use to strengthen their security posture.

The current release, **CIS Controls v8.1**, defines **18 top-level controls** supported by **153 safeguards.** These safeguards (formerly *subcontrols*) are tailored to three **Implementation Groups (IG1, IG2, IG3)** depending on organizational size, risk profile, and available resources.

CIS Critical Security Controls v8.1 Overview

The controls are grouped by **security function** as follows:

#	Control Name	Security Function
01	Inventory and Control of Enterprise Assets	Identify
02	Inventory and Control of Software Assets	Identify
03	Data Protection	Protect

04	Secure Configuration of Enterprise Assets & Software	Protect
05	Account Management	Protect
06	Access Control Management	Protect
07	Continuous Vulnerability Management	Protect
08	Audit Log Management	Detect
09	Email and Web Browser Protections	Protect
10	Malware Defenses	Protect
11	Data Recovery	Recover
12	Network Infrastructure Management	Protect
13	Security Awareness and Skills Training	Protect
14	Security Operations Center (SOC)	Detect
15	Service Provider Management	Govern
16	Application Software Security	Protect
17	Incident Response Management	Respond
18	Penetration Testing	Verify

APPENDIX B

NIST SP 800-53 Revision 5 Control Families

The **NIST Special Publication (SP) 800-53 Rev. 5** provides a **comprehensive catalog of security and privacy controls** for federal information systems and organizations. It supports **risk management**, ensures **FISMA compliance**, and aligns with other frameworks such as the **NIST Cybersecurity Framework** and **NIST Privacy Framework**.

Overview of Control Families

NIST organizes its catalog into **20 control families**, each addressing a distinct security or privacy domain:

Family Code	Control Family Name
AC	Access Control
AT	Awareness and Training
AU	Audit and Accountability
CA	Assessment, Authorization, and Monitoring
CM	Configuration Management

CP	Contingency Planning
IA	Identification and Authentication
IR	Incident Response
MA	Maintenance
MP	Media Protection
PE	Physical and Environmental Protection
PL	Planning
PS	Personnel Security
RA	Risk Assessment
SA	System and Services Acquisition
SC	System and Communications Protection
SI	System and Information Integrity
SR	Supply Chain Risk Management
PM	Program Management
PT	Privacy

Each family includes **base controls** and **control enhancements**. Enhancements add depth or specificity, supporting **higher assurance levels** or specialized use cases. Controls are selected based on system impact levels (*Low, Moderate, High*) and organizational needs.

NIST SP 800-53 Rev. 5.1.1: Control Families with Enhancements

The **Rev. 5.1.1 update** expands on this catalog, offering refined **controls and enhancements**, organized under the same 20 families. Below is a structured sample:

Family	Example Control	Enhancements (Sample)
AC – Access Control	AC-02: Account Management	AC-02(01): Automated System Account Management; AC-02(07): Role-Based Schemes
AT – Awareness and Training	AT-02: Literacy and Training	AT-02(02): Role-Based Training; AT-02(03): Insider Threat Awareness
AU – Audit and Accountability	AU-06: Audit Review & Reporting	AU-06(01): Process Integration; AU-06(03): Correlation with Physical Monitoring
CA – Assessment & Monitoring	CA-07: Continuous Monitoring	CA-07(01): Independent Assessment; CA-07(02): Automated Tools
CM – Configuration Management	CM-06: Configuration Settings	CM-06(01): Automated Enforcement; CM-06(02): Review and Update
CP – Contingency Planning	CP-09: System Backup	CP-09(01): Backup Integrity Testing; CP-09(02): Redundant Storage
IA – Identification & Authentication	IA-02: User Identification	IA-02(01): Multi-Factor Authentication; IA-02(07): Cryptographic Authentication

IR – Incident Response	IR-04: Incident Handling	IR-04(01): Automated Handling; IR-04(03): External Coordination
MA – Maintenance	MA-04: Nonlocal Maintenance	MA-04(01): Approval & Monitoring; MA-04(02): Cryptographic Protection
MP – Media Protection	MP-05: Media Transport	MP-05(01): Cryptographic Protection; MP-05(02): Manual Inspection
PE – Physical & Environmental	PE-03: Physical Access Control	PE-03(01): Transmission Medium Access; PE-03(03): Visitor Control
PL – Planning	PL-02: Security & Privacy Plans	PL-02(01): Plan Update; PL-02(02): Component Coverage
PS – Personnel Security	PS-03: Personnel Screening	PS-03(01): Risk-Based Screening; PS-03(02): Re-Screening
RA – Risk Assessment	RA-05: Vulnerability Scanning	RA-05(01): Vulnerability Updates; RA-05(02): Automated Trend Analysis
SA – System/Services Acquisition	SA-11: Developer Testing	SA-11(01): Independent Verification; SA-11(02): Code Analysis
SC – Communications Protection	SC-12: Key Establishment	SC-12(01): Automated Key Management; SC-12(02): Hardware-Based Protection
SI – System & Information Integrity	SI-04: Monitoring	SI-04(01): Automated Tools; SI-04(04): Traffic Monitoring
SR – Supply Chain Risk Mgmt.	SR-06: Supplier Reviews	SR-06(01): Independent Assessments; SR-06(02): Continuous Monitoring

PM – Program Management	PM-12: Insider Threat Program	PM-12(01): Integration with SOC; PM-12(02): Behavioral Indicators
PT – Privacy	PT-05: Minimization of PII	PT-05(01): Data Retention Limits; PT-05(02): Automated Minimization

The **complete catalog**, including downloadable spreadsheets and OSCAL formats, is available on the official **NIST SP 800-53 Rev. 5.1.1 site.**

APPENDIX C

ISO/IEC 27001:2022 Framework

The **ISO/IEC 27001:2022** standard defines a globally recognized framework for establishing, implementing, maintaining, and continually improving an **Information Security Management System (ISMS)**.

At its core is **Annex A**, which provides a structured set of **93 controls**—streamlined from the 114 controls in the 2013 edition. These controls are grouped into **four thematic categories**:

ISO/IEC 27001:2022 Control Themes

Theme	Description
Organizational	Governance, risk management, policies, operational procedures
People	Human resource security and awareness
Physical	Safeguarding physical assets and environments
Technological	Technical security for systems, networks, and applications

Organizational Controls (37 Controls)

These controls emphasize governance, risk, and operational management.

Control ID	Title	Purpose
A.5.1	Policies for information security	Define and communicate security policies
A.5.2	Information security roles and responsibilities	Assign and document responsibilities
A.5.3	Segregation of duties	Prevent conflicts of interest, reduce risk
A.5.4	Contact with authorities	Maintain engagement with regulators
A.5.5	Contact with special interest groups	Collaborate with industry bodies
A.5.6	Security in project management	Integrate controls into project lifecycles
A.5.7	Threat intelligence	Use threat data to inform decisions
A.5.8	Supplier relationship security	Manage third-party risks
A.5.9	Supplier agreements	Define contractual security requirements
A.5.10	ICT supply chain security	Secure supply chain dependencies

A.5.11	Supplier termination security	Enforce secure vendor off-boarding
A.5.12	Classification of information	Categorize data by sensitivity
A.5.13	Labeling of information	Mark data appropriately
A.5.14	Handling of information	Define secure use of data
A.5.15	Access control	Restrict access by role/policy
A.5.16	Identity management	Securely manage identities
A.5.17	Authentication information	Protect credentials
A.5.18	Access rights	Grant/revoke access systematically
A.5.19	Security in application development	Embed security in SDLC
A.5.20	Secure coding	Apply secure coding practices
A.5.21	Security testing in development	Validate before deployment
A.5.22	Protection of test data	Secure data in test environments
A.5.23	Information deletion	Securely erase data
A.5.24	Data masking	Obscure sensitive data in testing
A.5.25	Data leakage prevention	Prevent unauthorized transfer
A.5.26	Monitoring activities	Monitor user/system activity

A.5.27	Protection against malware	Detect and block malicious code
A.5.28	Technical vulnerability management	Patch and mitigate flaws
A.5.29	Configuration management	Maintain secure configurations
A.5.30	Information deletion (**duplicate of A.5.23 in source**)	*(Recommend consolidation with A.5.23)*
A.5.31	Backup	Ensure reliable data recovery
A.5.32	Logging	Record system events
A.5.33	Clock synchronization	Align system times for audit accuracy
A.5.34	Software installation	Control and authorize deployments
A.5.35	Use of cryptography	Protect data confidentiality/integrity
A.5.36	Key management	Secure management of cryptographic keys
A.5.37	Secure disposal/reuse of equipment	Prevent leakage from retired assets

People Controls (8 Controls)

These focus on workforce-related risks and awareness.

Control ID	Title	Purpose
A.6.1	Screening	Vet personnel before access
A.6.2	Terms and conditions of employment	Define contractual responsibilities
A.6.3	Security awareness & training	Build a security-conscious culture
A.6.4	Disciplinary process	Enforce consequences for violations
A.6.5	Post-employment responsibilities	Revoke access and protect assets
A.6.6	Confidentiality agreements	Safeguard sensitive information legally
A.6.7	Remote working	Secure offsite environments
A.6.8	Acceptable use policy	Define proper system/data use

Physical Controls (14 Controls – Theme A.7)

These controls safeguard physical environments, equipment, and supporting infrastructure.

Control ID	Title	Purpose
A.7.1	Security perimeter	Define secure boundaries
A.7.2	Physical entry	Regulate entry to secure areas
A.7.3	Securing offices/facilities	Lock, monitor, and control access
A.7.4	Environmental threat protection	Mitigate fire, flood, power risks
A.7.5	Secure area operations	Establish rules for sensitive zones
A.7.6	Delivery/loading areas	Control ingress/egress points
A.7.7	Equipment placement/protection	Position IT hardware securely
A.7.8	Off-premises asset security	Safeguard mobile equipment/data
A.7.9	Storage media	Protect removable/non-removable media
A.7.10	Supporting utilities	Ensure resilience of power/cooling
A.7.11	Cabling security	Protect against tampering/interference
A.7.12	Equipment maintenance	Authorize and monitor upkeep
A.7.13	Removal of assets	Control disposal/transfer securely

A.7.14	Unattended user equipment	Safeguard temporarily unattended devices

Technological Controls (36 Controls – Theme A.8)

These controls enforce technical safeguards for systems, applications, and cloud environments.

Control ID	Title	Purpose
A.8.1	User endpoint devices	Secure laptops, mobiles, endpoints
A.8.2	Privileged access rights	Restrict and monitor admin rights
A.8.3	Information access restriction	Enforce access policies
A.8.4	Source code access	Control code repository access
A.8.5	Secure authentication	Implement strong mechanisms
A.8.6	Capacity management	Ensure secure system performance
A.8.7	Malware protection	Deploy antimalware controls
A.8.8	Technical vulnerability management	Identify and remediate flaws
A.8.9	Configuration management	Maintain consistent security baselines
A.8.10	Information deletion	Secure data erasure

A.8.11	Data masking	Obscure sensitive test/analytical data
A.8.12	Data leakage prevention	Prevent unauthorized exfiltration
A.8.13	Information backup	Ensure secure data recoverability
A.8.14	Processing redundancy	Maintain availability via failover
A.8.15	Logging	Record system/user activity
A.8.16	Monitoring activities	Continuous threat detection
A.8.17	Clock synchronization	Ensure time consistency for logs
A.8.18	Use of cryptography	Encrypt data in transit and at rest
A.8.19	Key management	Protect cryptographic key lifecycle
A.8.20	Network security	Secure networks from threats
A.8.21	Network services security	Harden service configurations
A.8.22	Network segregation	Isolate critical systems/data
A.8.23	Web filtering	Control user web access
A.8.24	Mobile device use	Apply mobile security policies
A.8.25	Teleworking	Protect remote work environments
A.8.26	Application security requirements	Define security in SDLC
A.8.27	Secure architecture principles	Apply security by design

A.8.28	Secure coding	Enforce development standards
A.8.29	Security testing	Validate controls pre-deployment
A.8.30	Protection of test data	Safeguard testing data sets
A.8.31	ICT supply chain	Manage supplier/third-party risks
A.8.32	Cloud service security	Ensure safe adoption of cloud
A.8.33	ICT readiness for continuity	Build resilience and recovery
A.8.34	Audit testing safeguards	Prevent disruptions/exposures

Summary

The **ISO/IEC 27001:2022 controls** provide a holistic approach to information security—addressing **governance, people, physical infrastructure, and technology**. Together, they form the foundation for an ISMS that is resilient, adaptable, and globally aligned with evolving cybersecurity challenges.

APPENDIX D

NIST Cybersecurity Framework (CSF) 2.0

The **NIST Cybersecurity Framework** (CSF)—now in **version 2.0**—does not prescribe fixed "controls" like NIST SP 800-53. Instead, it defines a structured model of **Functions, Categories, and Subcategories** that represent desired cybersecurity outcomes. These outcomes can be **mapped to prescriptive controls** in standards such as **NIST SP 800-53 Rev. 5, ISO/IEC 27001:2022 Annex A**, or **CIS Controls.**

NIST CSF 2.0 Structure

- **Functions:** 6 high-level cybersecurity activities
- **Categories:** 22 subdivisions of Functions
- **Subcategories:** 106 specific outcomes

Functions and Categories

- **Govern**
  - Organizational Context
  - Risk Management Strategy
  - Cybersecurity Supply Chain Risk Management
  - Roles, Responsibilities, and Authorities

- Policy
- Oversight
- Cybersecurity Program Management

- **Identify**
  - Asset Management
  - Risk Assessment
  - Data Management
- **Protect**
  - Identity Management, Authentication, and Access Control
  - Awareness and Training
  - Platform Security
  - Data Security
  - Protective Technology
- **Detect**
  - Anomalies and Events
  - Continuous Monitoring
  - Detection Processes
- **Respond**
  - Incident Management
  - Incident Analysis
  - Incident Response Reporting & Communication
  - Incident Mitigation

    - Incident Recovery
- **Recover**
    - Recovery Plan Execution
    - Improvements
    - Communication

Example Mappings (CSF ↔ NIST SP 800-53 ↔ ISO/IEC 27001:2022)

CSF Function	Category	Subcategory Example	NIST SP 800-53 Control(s)	ISO/IEC 27001:2022 Control(s)
Protect	PR.IP	PR.IP6: Data is destroyed according to policy	MP-6 (Media Sanitization), SR-12 (Component Disposal)	A.8.3 (Information deletion), A.7.4 (Media handling)
Identify	ID.AM	ID.AM1: Physical devices and systems are inventoried	CM-8 (System Component Inventory)	A.5.9 (Asset Inventory)
Detect	DE.CM	DE.CM1: Network monitoring is performed	AU-12 (Audit Generation), SI-4 (Monitoring)	A.5.7 (Monitoring activities)
Respond	RS.CO	RS.CO2: Incidents are reported to stakeholders	IR-6 (Incident Reporting), IR-4 (Incident Handling)	A.5.24 (Incident Management)

Govern	GV.RR	GV.RR1: Roles and responsibilities are defined	PM-3 (Security Resources), AT-1 (Awareness Policy)	A.5.1 (Leadership commitment), A.5.3 (Roles & Authorities)

These mappings—maintained in **NIST OLIR** and ISO crosswalk resources—help organizations **link strategic outcomes to operational controls**, improving governance, audit readiness, and dashboard alignment.

APPENDIX E

Capability Maturity Model Integration (CMMI)

The **Capability Maturity Model Integration (CMMI)**, developed by Carnegie Mellon University and maintained by ISACA, is a **globally recognized framework** for assessing and improving organizational **process maturity, performance, and resilience.**

Key Objectives

- Drive **process improvement** across projects, services, and acquisitions
- Benchmark **capability and performance**
- Reduce risk and improve efficiency
- Align operations with **business goals** and **customer expectations**
- CMMI can be applied in two representations:
- **Staged:** overall organizational maturity
- **Continuous:** capability maturity in specific process areas

CMMI Maturity Levels

Level	Name	Description
1 – Initial	Processes are ad hoc, chaotic, reactive; success depends on individuals	
2 – Managed	Basic project management processes are established; work tracked	
3 – Defined	Organization-wide standards and proactive process management	
4 – Quantitatively Managed	Processes measured, controlled, and data-driven	
5 – Optimizing	Continuous improvement and innovation; proactive refinement	

Practice Areas span governance, planning, quality assurance, business resilience, and engineering disciplines.

APPENDIX F

Federal Information Security Modernization Act (FISMA)

The **Federal Information Security Modernization Act** (FISMA) establishes requirements for U.S. federal agencies to implement **comprehensive information security programs.**

A common evaluation tool is the **FISMA Matrix**, used to measure compliance with **NIST SP 800-53** and align security activities with the **NIST Cybersecurity Framework** (CSF).

Purpose of a FISMA Matrix

- Map controls to **NIST SP 800-53** requirements
- Align agency functions with **CSF (Govern, Identify, Protect, Detect, Respond, Recover)**
- Evaluate maturity in governance, risk, supply chain, and technical safeguards
- Support Inspector General (IG) and CIO reporting for annual FISMA audits

Example Structure of a FISMA Matrix

Function	Domain	Metrics Evaluated
Govern	Cybersecurity Governance	Policies, roles, oversight mechanisms
Identify	Risk & Asset Management	Inventory, classification, risk assessments
Protect	Configuration & Access Mgmt	Baselines, IAM, data protection
Detect	Continuous Monitoring	Logging, alerting, anomaly detection
Respond	Incident Response	Plans, playbooks, stakeholder coordination
Recover	Contingency Planning	Backups, recovery, continuity strategies

These matrices are often implemented in **CyberScope** and referenced in **OMB, DHS, and Congressional reports,** providing agencies with structured compliance visibility.

APPENDIX G

Risk Management Framework (RMF)

The **Risk Management Framework** (**RMF**), developed by NIST under **FISMA**, provides a **structured, repeatable methodology** for managing security and privacy risks in federal information systems. It integrates safeguards into the **System Development Life Cycle** (**SDLC**) and is formally outlined in **NIST SP 800-37 Rev. 2**.

Seven Steps of RMF

Step	Purpose	Significance to Enterprise Security
1. Prepare	Establish context, assign roles, define risk tolerance	Builds governance foundation, resource allocation, and readiness
2. Categorize	Classify systems/data by impact (per FIPS 199)	Ensures protection aligned to confidentiality, integrity, and availability
3. Select	Choose baseline controls (NIST SP 800-53) by impact/risk	Aligns safeguards with enterprise risk appetite and threat landscape
4. Implement	Apply and document selected controls	Operationalizes safeguards across technical, administrative, and physical layers

5. Assess	Evaluate control effectiveness	Confirms safeguards function as intended and highlights gaps
6. Authorize	Senior officials grant risk-based approval	Establishes accountability and acceptance of residual risk
7. Monitor	Continuously track control performance and threats	Enables adaptive posture, continuous compliance, and resilience

Why RMF Matters

- Integrates security **early** in the SDLC
- Supports **risk-based decision-making**
- Enables **continuous monitoring and adaptation**
- Aligns with **FISMA, NIST SP 800-53, and NIST CSF**
- Provides assurance for **audit readiness** and achieving **Authorization to Operate (ATO)**

APPENDIX H

Enterprise Email Usage Policy

Policy Title: Enterprise Email Usage Policy

Version: 1.0

Effective Date: August 1, 2025

Approved By: Chief Information Security Officer (CISO)

Applies To: Employees, contractors, and third parties using enterprise email systems

This policy aligns with **ISO/IEC 27001:2022 controls** (A.8.9, A.5.15, A.6.8) and **NIST SP 800-53 controls** (AC-17, SC-12, SI-4).

1. Purpose

To ensure secure, professional, and compliant use of enterprise email systems. The policy protects sensitive data, reduces breach risk, and enforces alignment with organizational and regulatory requirements.

2. Scope

- All enterprise-provided accounts (e.g., *@company.com*)
- All devices (desktop, mobile, remote) accessing enterprise email

- All business-related communications

3. Acceptable Use

- Use email strictly for authorized business purposes
- Maintain professionalism; avoid offensive/discriminatory content
- Encrypt sensitive transmissions (TLS, S/MIME)
- Use only **approved email clients**
- Include **disclaimers/confidentiality notices** where required

4. Prohibited Activities

- Personal gain, politics, or illegal purposes
- Chain letters, spam, or bulk unsolicited mail
- Sending unencrypted confidential data
- Auto-forwarding to personal accounts
- Circumventing email security controls

5. Security Requirements

- **Authentication:** Multi-factor authentication (MFA) mandatory
- **Encryption:** Sensitive communications encrypted end-to-end
- **Malware Protection:** Attachments scanned; suspicious items reported
- **Phishing:** Mandatory awareness training; suspected attempts reported

- **Monitoring:** Traffic monitored for compliance, threats, and audit

6. Retention & Archiving

- Retained per data retention policy
- Emails under legal hold must not be deleted
- Automated archiving; manual archiving requires authorization

7. Compliance & Enforcement

- Violations may lead to:
- Suspension of privileges
- Disciplinary action, up to termination
- Legal consequences if applicable

8. Related Policies

- Information Classification Policy
- Data Protection & Privacy Policy
- Acceptable Use Policy
- ISO/IEC 27001:2022 (Annex A references)
- NIST SP 800-53 (aligned controls)

9. Acknowledgment

All users must review and acknowledge this policy annually (signed or digital acceptance).

APPENDIX I

Open Systems Interconnection (OSI) Model

The **OSI Model,** created by ISO, provides a **seven-layer conceptual framework** that standardizes communication in telecom and computing systems. It supports interoperability, structured troubleshooting, and targeted security mapping.

Purpose of OSI Model

- **Standardization:** Creates a universal reference for network operations
- **Modularity:** Breaks complex processes into distinct layers
- **Interoperability:** Enables multi-vendor system communication
- **Security Mapping:** Identifies vulnerabilities at each network layer

The Seven Layers & Security Considerations

Layer	Name	Function	Security Considerations
7	Application	User-facing applications (browsers, email)	Input validation, authentication, malware scanning

6	Presentation	Data translation, encryption/decryption	TLS/SSL, secure encoding
5	Session	Manages sessions between apps	Session hijack prevention, timeout enforcement
4	Transport	Reliable data transfer (TCP/UDP)	Port filtering, DoS prevention, secure protocols
3	Network	Routing, IP addressing	IPsec, firewalls, anti-spoofing
2	Data Link	Node-to-node delivery, MAC addressing	VLANs, MAC filtering, ARP spoof defense
1	Physical	Transmission over media (cables, radio)	Physical access controls, tamper detection

Practical Applications in Security

- **Defense-in-Depth:** Safeguards applied per layer
- **Threat Mapping:** e.g., MAC spoofing at Layer 2, SYN floods at Layer 4, malware injection at Layer 7
- **Security Tools:** NAC & physical controls (L1–2), Firewalls/IDS/VPN (L3–4), WAF/DLP/Endpoint Protection (L5–7)

Control Mapping – OSI vs. ISO 27001 & NIST SP 800-53

OSI Layer	ISO/IEC 27001:2022 Controls	NIST SP 800-53 Rev. 5 Controls
Layer 1: Physical	A.7.4, A.7.5, A.7.8	PE-01, PE-03, PE-06

Layer 2: Data Link	A.8.9, A.8.10	SC-07, SC-12, AC-04
Layer 3: Network	A.8.20, A.8.23	AC-17, SC-07, SC-32
Layer 4: Transport	A.8.24, A.8.28	SC-08, SC-12, AC-19
Layer 5: Session	A.8.27, A.8.28	AC-11, SC-10, IA-02
Layer 6: Presentation	A.8.25, A.8.26	SC-12, SC-13, SI-10
Layer 7: Application	A.5.1, A.6.1, A.8.9	PL-02, SI-04, AU-06

Use Cases for Training & Audit

- **Training Modules:** Layer-based attack scenarios + mapped controls
- **Audit Prep:** Validate defense coverage across all layers; identify gaps
- **Executive Dashboards:** Visualize layered safeguards for governance and compliance

APPENDIX J

Payment Card Industry Data Security Standard (PCI DSS)

The **Payment Card Industry Data Security Standard** (**PCI DSS**) defines global requirements for protecting cardholder data across its lifecycle. Below is a structured overview of the **current version**, its application, and a step-by-step auditing guide tailored for governance and cybersecurity professionals.

Current Version of PCI DSS

- **PCI DSS v4.0.1 (Published June 2024)**
- Retired predecessor: **v4.0 (sunset on December 31, 2024)**
- **Key clarifications in v4.0.1:**
    - Refined applicability notes for issuers and service providers
    - Reverted critical patch timelines back to **30 days**
    - Updated guidance on **multi-factor authentication** (MFA)
    - Revised definitions (e.g., *Phishing Resistant Authentication, Visitor*)

Who Must Comply?

Organizations that store, process, or transmit cardholder data, including:

- Merchants
- Payment processors
- Financial institutions
- Service providers

Core Objectives:

- Protect cardholder data in storage, processing, and transmission
- Secure systems and networks
- Maintain governance and continuous monitoring

The 12 Core Requirements (Grouped into 6 Domains)

Domain	Requirement
Build & Maintain Secure Systems	1. Install and maintain network security controls 2. Apply secure configurations
Protect Cardholder Data	3. Protect stored data 4. Encrypt data in transit
Maintain Vulnerability Management	5. Protect against malware 6. Develop secure systems
Implement Strong Access Control	7. Restrict access 8. Authenticate users

	9. Restrict physical access
Monitor & Test Networks	10. Log and monitor access 11. Test security regularly
Maintain Security Policies	12. Establish and enforce security policies

Step-by-Step PCI DSS Audit Guide

1. **Define the Cardholder Data Environment (CDE)**
   - Map systems, networks, and third-party providers handling cardholder data.
   - Apply segmentation to isolate the CDE.
2. **Conduct Gap Analysis**
   - Compare current safeguards against v4.0.1 requirements.
   - Identify administrative, technical, and physical gaps.
3. **Remediate Gaps**
   - Apply missing controls (encryption, logging, access limits).
   - Update policies and train staff.
4. **Scope and Planning**
   - Define audit boundaries (systems, apps, service providers).
   - Reduce scope where feasible.
5. **Evidence Gathering**
   - Collect policies, configurations, logs, training records.
   - Use **SAQs (Self-Assessment Questionnaires)** and ROC templates.

6. **Onsite Assessment**
    - QSA (Qualified Security Assessor) validates compliance via interviews, observation, and testing.
7. **Report Delivery**
    - Receive **Report on Compliance (RoC)** and **Attestation of Compliance (AoC)**.
8. **Continuous Monitoring**
    - Maintain logging, annual assessments, and staff training.
9. **Strategic Governance Notes**
    - **Customized Approach**: PCI DSS v4.0.1 allows flexibility if objectives are met.
    - **Third-Party Risk:** Vendors handling cardholder data must also be PCI DSS compliant.
    - **Automation:** Use GRC platforms for evidence collection and compliance dashboards.

Recommended PCI DSS Audit Checklist Templates

1. **Cyber Arrow PCI DSS Checklist**
    - Format: Free template
    - Covers all 12 requirements with practical remediation steps
    - Best for: Roadmap-focused organizations
2. **Audit-Now PCI DSS Audit Checklist**
    - Format: PDF/Word
    - Control-by-control questions for financial & IT environments

- Best for: Internal auditors & compliance officers

3. **Safety Culture PCI Compliance Checklist**
   - Format: Digital (exportable)
   - Includes POS security checks, evidence upload, digital signatures
   - Best for: Retail audits
4. **Secure frame PCI DSS Hub**
   - Format: GRC toolkit
   - Includes Compliance Checklist, Attestation Template, Pen Test Review, Risk Assessment
   - Best for: Organizations seeking certification readiness

Pro Tip: Adapt these checklists into **dashboards** showing control status, responsible owners, evidence links, frequency, and risk ratings.

APPENDIX K

Health Insurance Portability and Accountability Act (HIPAA)

The **Health Insurance Portability and Accountability Act** (**HIPAA**), enacted in 1996, provides national standards for protecting **health information.** It applies to healthcare entities and their business associates, with compliance enforced through multiple rules and regular audits.

Current HIPAA Framework (2025)

Core Rules & Updates:

- **Privacy Rule (2003):** Governs PHI use/disclosure
- **Security Rule (2005):** Defines safeguards for ePHI
- **Breach Notification Rule (2009, via HITECH)**
- **Omnibus Rule (2013):** Expanded business associate accountability
- **Recent Updates (2024–2025):**
- Privacy Rule: Reproductive health protections (*vacated June 2025*)

- Security Rule: Proposed alignment with **HHS Healthcare Cybersecurity Strategy**
- Part 162: Streamlined claims & interoperability updates
- 42 CFR Part 2: Substance use disorder records integrated into HIPAA protections

Who Must Comply?

- **Covered Entities:**
  - Healthcare providers (transmitting health data electronically)
  - Health plans (insurers, HMOs)
  - Clearinghouses
- **Business Associates:**
  - Vendors handling PHI (billing, analytics, cloud storage)

What HIPAA Protects

- **PHI**: Protected Health Information (oral, paper, electronic)
- **ePHI**: Electronic PHI (subject to Security Rule)

Audit Steps for HIPAA Compliance

1. **Assign Officers**
   - Designate Privacy & Security Officers for oversight.
2. **Conduct Risk Analysis**
   - Identify threats, assess likelihood/impact, document mitigation.
3. **Review Policies & Procedures**

- Validate policies for **access control, transmission, training, incident response.**
- Update policies to reflect new 2025 changes.

4. **Evaluate Safeguards**
    - **Administrative:** Training, periodic risk assessments
    - **Physical:** Facility access, workstation security
    - **Technical:** Encryption, logs, MFA
5. **Train Workforce**
    - Annual HIPAA training including breach reporting & PHI handling.
6. **Document PHI Inventory**
    - Catalog systems, devices, and transmission points.
7. **Audit Business Associate Agreements (BAAs)**
    - Verify all vendors have signed BAAs with compliance clauses.
8. **Perform Internal Audit**
    - Review compliance with Privacy, Security, Breach Rules.
    - Identify non-conformities & corrective measures.
9. **Prepare for OCR Audit**
    - Maintain documentation: risk assessments, incident reports, policies, training logs.
10. **Monitor & Update**
    - Annual reviews and policy updates based on **regulatory changes.**

APPENDIX L

The General Data Protection Regulation (GDPR)

The **General Data Protection Regulation** (**GDPR**), formally **Regulation** (**EU**) **2016/679**, was adopted in **April 2016** and became enforceable on **May 25, 2018**. It replaces **Directive 95/46/EC** and applies directly to all EU member states. The consolidated version includes corrections from **OJ L 127** (**23 May 2018**), but no major amendments have been introduced since its enactment.

Application of GDPR

Who Must Comply?

GDPR applies to:

- **EU-based organizations** processing personal data.
- **Non-EU organizations** offering goods or services to, or monitoring the behavior of, EU residents.

What GDPR Protects:

- **Personal Data:** Any information identifying a natural person (e.g., name, email, IP address).

- **Special Categories of Data:** Includes health, biometric, racial, political, and religious data, requiring enhanced safeguards.

Key Roles Under GDPR

Role	Responsibility
Data Controller	Determines the purpose and means of processing personal data.
Data Processor	Processes personal data on behalf of the controller.
Data Protection Officer (DPO)	Oversees compliance, advises staff, and liaises with supervisory authorities.

Step-by-Step Guide to Auditing GDPR Compliance

1. **Define Scope and Objectives**
    - Identify systems, departments, and third parties involved in data processing.
    - Set audit objectives: compliance verification, risk assessment, and remediation planning.
2. **Map Data Flows**
    - Document collection, storage, use, and transfer of personal data.
    - Include categories, sources, retention, and access permissions.
3. **Perform Data Inventory**
    - Catalog personal and sensitive data types (customers, employees, vendors).
    - Identify lawful basis (e.g., consent, contract, legal obligation).
4. **Assess Data Protection Measures**

- Evaluate **technical controls** (encryption, backups, access restrictions).
- Review **organizational safeguards** (training, breach reporting, DPIAs).

5. **Review Third-Party Contracts**
    - Confirm GDPR-compliant **Data Processing Agreements (DPAs)**.
    - Verify privacy and security obligations in vendor contracts.
6. **Verify Documentation**
    - Ensure availability of: ROPA (Records of Processing Activities), privacy notices, consent logs, DPIAs, and breach records.
7. **Conduct Interviews & Testing**
    - Interview IT, HR, Legal, Marketing.
    - Test access controls, retention, and incident response.
8. **Identify Gaps and Risks**
    - Compare practices against **GDPR Articles and Recitals.**
    - Rank findings by severity and potential fines (up to **€20M or 4% of global turnover**).
9. **Develop Remediation Plan**
    - Assign owners, resources, and deadlines.
    - Update policies, provide training, and implement technical fixes.
10. **Monitor and Reassess**
    - Conduct annual or post-incident audits.

- Track remediation progress and maintain updated risk registers.

Governance Tips

- Integrate GDPR within **ISO 27001 and NIST CSF frameworks** for consistency.
- Use dashboards for compliance visualization and audit traceability.
- Apply **legal privilege structuring** for sensitive findings to protect confidentiality.

APPENDIX M

The California Consumer Privacy Act (CCPA)

The **California Consumer Privacy Act (CCPA)**, enacted in **2018** and effective **January 1, 2020**, grants California residents enhanced rights over their personal data. The **California Privacy Rights Act (CPRA)**, effective **January 1, 2023**, amended and expanded CCPA. Today, the **California Privacy Protection Agency (CPPA)** oversees enforcement and rulemaking.

Current Version (2025)

- **CCPA as amended by CPRA** governs compliance.
- **Recent Updates (2025):**
- Mandatory **annual cybersecurity audits** for high-risk processing.
- **Risk assessments** required for profiling and automated decision-making.
- Expanded protections for **sensitive personal information.**
- Final regulations expected by **Q4 2025.**

Who Must Comply?

CCPA applies to for-profit businesses meeting any one of the following:

- **Annual revenue > $25 million.**
- Processing data of **100,000+ consumers or households.**
- Deriving **≥50% revenue** from selling or sharing personal data.

What CCPA Protects

- **Personal Information:** Names, emails, geolocation, IP addresses, biometrics.
- **Sensitive Personal Information:** SSNs, financial data, race, health, precise geolocation.

Consumer Rights under CCPA/CPRA:

Right	Description
Know	Right to know what personal data is collected and shared.
Delete	Right to request deletion of personal data.
Opt-Out	Right to opt out of the sale or sharing of personal data.
Correct	Right to correct inaccurate personal data.
Limit	Right to restrict the use of sensitive personal data.
Non-Discrimination	Right to equal service regardless of exercising privacy rights.

Step-by-Step Guide to Auditing CCPA Compliance

1. **Determine Applicability**
    - Confirm thresholds are met.
    - Include subsidiaries and service providers in scope.
2. **Map Data Flows**

- Track all personal data collection, storage, and transfers from California residents.

3. **Conduct Data Inventory**
    - Classify personal vs. sensitive data.
    - Record collection methods (web forms, cookies, APIs).
4. **Review Privacy Policies**
    - Ensure policies disclose: categories of data, retention, rights, opt-out mechanisms.
5. **Assess Consumer Rights Mechanisms**
    - Validate presence of **opt-out links/banners**.
    - Test request handling for access, correction, and deletion.
6. **Evaluate Security Controls**
    - Check encryption, IAM, and breach response plans.
    - Align with **CPRA cybersecurity audit mandates**.
7. **Audit Vendor Contracts**
    - Confirm Data Processing Agreements (DPAs) with third parties.
    - Verify downstream obligations.
8. **Train Employees**
    - Provide role-based privacy training.
    - Track completion and comprehension.
9. **Document & Remediate**

- Record audit findings, assign owners, and set remediation timelines.

10. Monitor & Update

- Conduct annual audits.
- Track regulatory updates (via CPPA guidance).

Governance Insights

- Integrate CCPA audits with **ISO 27001 and NIST CSF** frameworks.
- Use automated tools for **consent management, data mapping, and DSR tracking.**
- Build executive dashboards for **consumer request metrics, compliance status, and risk exposure**.

Recommended CCPA Audit Checklist Templates (2025)

1. **Securiti – CCPA Compliance Checklist**
   - Covers applicability criteria, consent notices, rights metrics, vendor disclosures.
   - Best for: Structured governance roadmaps.
2. **SafeAeon – CCPA Audit Checklist (2024 Guide)**
   - Breaks down seven consumer rights.
   - Best for: Internal privacy/security teams.
3. **Workable – CCPA Compliance Checklist (PDF)**
   - Quick-reference with data handling and consumer request validation.

- Best for: Fast audit preparation.

Governance Tip

Adapt templates into **compliance dashboards** tracking:

- Control status
- Evidence & ownership
- Consumer rights request metrics
- Risk scores & remediation progress

APPENDIX N

GRC (Governance, Risk Management, and Compliance)

What is GRC?

GRC, which stands for Governance, Risk Management, and Compliance, is a strategic framework that integrates oversight, risk mitigation, and regulatory alignment within an organization's operations—particularly in cybersecurity.

Core Pillars:

Pillar	Description
Governance	Defines roles, responsibilities, and decision-making structures for security.
Risk Management	Identifies, assesses, and mitigates cyber risks across systems and assets.
Compliance	Ensures adherence to laws, standards (e.g., GDPR, HIPAA, ISO 27001), and policies.

Why GRC Matters to Security Enterprises

1. **Strategic Alignment**

- Aligns cybersecurity initiatives with business goals and risk appetite.
- Promotes executive-level accountability and cross-functional collaboration.

2. **Risk Visibility and Prioritization**
    - Enables proactive identification of threats such as phishing, insider risk, and supply chain vulnerabilities.
    - Supports risk-based decision-making and resource allocation.
3. **Regulatory Compliance**
    - Helps meet evolving legal obligations, such as CCPA, NIS2, and DORA.
    - Reduces exposure to fines, audits, and reputational damage.
4. **Operational Resilience**
    - Embeds security into business processes rather than just IT silos.
    - Facilitates incident response, business continuity, and breach recovery.
5. **Enterprise-Wide Accountability**
    - Expands responsibility beyond IT to include legal, HR, and executive leadership.
    - Fosters a culture of security and ethical behavior.

GRC vs Traditional Cybersecurity

Aspect	Traditional Cybersecurity	GRC-Driven Cybersecurity
Focus	Threat detection and response	Business risk, compliance, governance
Responsibility	IT or security team	Shared across departments and leadership
Strategy	Technical tools and firewalls	Strategic alignment with business goals
Compliance	Reactive fixes	Proactive audits and certifications
Documentation	Tool-specific logs	Enterprise-wide reporting and accountability

APPENDIX O

The NIS2 Directive

The NIS2 Directive is an EU-wide legal framework designed to enhance cybersecurity and resilience across essential and vital organizations within the European Union. Replacing the original NIS Directive, it introduces stricter requirements for cybersecurity risk management and incident reporting. Member States are required to transpose the directive into national law by **October 17, 2024**.

Purpose and Scope:

- **Enhance Cybersecurity**
    - NIS2 aims to elevate the overall level of cybersecurity across the EU by setting minimum standards for organizations and critical infrastructure.
- **Harmonization**
    - It seeks to harmonize cybersecurity practices across the EU, reducing fragmentation and fostering cross-border cooperation.

- **Essential and Important Entities**
    - The directive applies to essential entities such as energy, transport, and banking, as well as important entities like digital providers and waste management.
- **Critical Infrastructure**
    - NIS2 focuses on protecting critical infrastructure and services that are vital to the economy and society.

Key Requirements:

- **Risk Management**
    - Organizations must implement comprehensive cybersecurity risk management measures, including incident handling, supply chain security, and access control.
- **Incident Reporting**
    - NIS2 introduces stricter incident reporting obligations, requiring entities to report significant cybersecurity incidents to relevant authorities.
- **Supervision and Enforcement**
    - Member States are responsible for supervising and enforcing the directive's requirements, with penalties for non-compliance.

Key Changes from NIS1:

Feature	NIS1	NIS2 (2022/2555)
Scope	Limited sectors	18 sectors including healthcare, cloud, public administration
Enforcement	National discretion	Harmonized EU-wide audits & penalties
Risk Management	General guidance	Specific technical & organizational measures
Incident Reporting	Major incidents only	24-hour early warning + detailed follow-up
Accountability	Operational level	Executive-level liability for non-compliance

Application of NIS2

Who Must Comply?

- **Essential Entities:** Large organizations in critical sectors (e.g. energy, transport, finance, healthcare).
- **Important Entities:** Medium-sized organizations in sectors like digital infrastructure, cloud, public services.
- **Covered Sectors (Annex I & II)**
- Energy, transport, banking, healthcare, digital infrastructure.
- Public administration, postal services, waste management, space sector.

Core Requirements:

- Risk assessments and security policies
- Supply chain security and vendor oversight
- Incident response and business continuity planning
- Encryption, MFA, and secure system design

NIS2 Compliance Audit Guide

Step-by-Step Audit Framework

1. **Governance & Risk Management**
    - Assign NIS2 compliance roles (e.g., CISO, board oversight).
    - Define risk appetite and document cyber risks.
    - Ensure executive accountability for cybersecurity decisions.
2. **Cybersecurity Policies & Procedures**
    - Maintain documented security policies and incident response plans.
    - Implement ticketing systems for incident triage and reporting.
    - Secure supply chain interactions and disaster recovery plans.
3. **Technical & Operational Controls**
    - Conduct vulnerability assessments and patch management.
    - Use encryption for data at rest and in transit.
    - Deploy endpoint protection and secure network architecture.
4. **Supply Chain Security**
    - Identify critical suppliers and assess their security posture.

- Include cybersecurity clauses in contracts.
- Monitor third-party risks and response capabilities.

5. **Incident Reporting**
   - Develop a formal incident response plan.
   - Train staff on detection and reporting protocols.
   - Ensure 24-hour early warning and follow-up reporting to CSIRTs.
6. **Legal & Regulatory Mapping**
   - Align NIS2 with GDPR, ISO 27001, NIST SP 800-53.
   - Maintain documentation of compliance efforts.
   - Review policies regularly for regulatory updates.
7. **Personnel & Training**
   - Conduct role-based cybersecurity training.
   - Implement access controls and MFA for privileged users.
   - Promote awareness of phishing and social engineering risks.
8. **Continuous Monitoring & Improvement**
   - Schedule internal audits and penetration tests.
   - Maintain a compliance dashboard mapped to Article 21 controls.
   - Participate in peer reviews and EU-wide threat sharing initiatives.

APPENDIX P

The Digital Operational Resilience Act (DORA)

Overview of DORA

The **Digital Operational Resilience Act (DORA)**, Regulation EU 2022/2554, represents a critical European Union initiative designed to manage **ICT (Information and Communication Technology) risks** in the financial sector. The regulation aims to ensure that financial entities can effectively **withstand, respond to, and recover** from cyberattacks, system failures, and other digital disruptions.

In simple terms, **DORA** seeks to secure the digital infrastructure that supports financial entities such as banks, insurers, and investment firms. It mandates that these institutions implement standardized measures for **protecting, detecting, containing, and recovering** from ICT-related disruptions. With a focus on financial entities, DORA also extends to third-party **ICT service providers** that play a pivotal role in these operations.

Key Dates

- **Adopted:** November 2022
- **Effective Date:** January 17, 2025

- **Compliance Deadline:** January 17, 2025

Application Scope

Who Must Comply?

The following entities are required to comply with DORA:

Entity Type	Examples
Financial Entities	Banks, insurers, investment firms, payment providers, crypto platforms
ICT Third-Party Providers	Cloud platforms, cybersecurity vendors, data centers
Critical Third-Party Providers (CTPPs)	Providers designated by EU regulators (EBA, ESMA, EIOPA) for direct oversight

Key Areas Covered by DORA:

- **ICT Risk Management:** Establishing a framework for managing ICT risks.
- **Incident Reporting:** Mandating timely reporting of digital disruptions.
- **Digital Resilience Testing:** Ensuring readiness for ICT-related challenges.
- **Third-Party Risk Oversight:** Managing security within third-party services.
- **Information Sharing (Voluntary):** Encouraging shared intelligence on cybersecurity threats.

DORA Compliance Audit Guide

This section outlines the key steps necessary to audit an organization's **DORA compliance:**

1. **Governance & Accountability**
    - Establish **board-level oversight** of ICT risks, ensuring that top leadership is responsible for resilience efforts.
    - Define clear **roles and responsibilities** for risk management (Article 5).
    - Allocate sufficient **budget and resources** for resilience measures, demonstrating commitment from the highest levels of management.
2. **ICT Risk Management Framework**
    - Document comprehensive **policies for risk identification, mitigation, and monitoring** to establish a systematic approach to addressing ICT threats.
    - Implement essential **access controls, encryption**, and **secure configurations** to safeguard systems and data.
    - Conduct **regular vulnerability scans** and **patch management** to mitigate potential risks from outdated systems.
3. **Incident Management**
    - Create a **detailed incident response plan** to define the steps to be taken when a cyber incident occurs.
    - Establish clear **escalation paths** and specific **reporting timelines:**

- Initial report: Within **4 hours**
- Intermediate report: Within **72 hours**
- Final report: Within **1 month**
- Ensure the **audit trails** are **tamper-proof**, allowing for reliable post-incident analysis.

4. **Digital Operational Resilience Testing**
   - Conduct **basic and advanced testing**, such as **Threat-Led Penetration Testing**, to assess the strength of the organization's defenses.
   - Evaluate **business continuity** and **disaster recovery plans** to ensure operational resilience in case of a digital disruption.
   - Document test results thoroughly and track **remediation actions** to close any gaps identified during testing.
5. **Third-Party Risk Management**
   - Maintain a comprehensive **register of ICT providers** to monitor the security posture of all third-party vendors.
   - Assess the **security posture of vendors** and include relevant **contractual clauses** to ensure compliance with DORA.
   - Continuously monitor **subcontracting and service dependencies** to identify any new risks arising from third-party relationships.

6. **Oversight of Critical ICT Providers**
    - Ensure contracts with **critical ICT providers** meet all DORA compliance requirements, including security standards and service continuity clauses.
    - Prepare for potential **audits** and **supervisory reviews** by relevant regulatory authorities.
    - Share **performance and incident data** with regulators to ensure transparency and regulatory oversight.
7. **Information Sharing (Optional)**
    - Actively engage in **threat intelligence exchange** to improve the collective defense against cyber threats.
    - Maintain records of **shared insights** and collaborative actions, contributing to the wider cybersecurity community.

Benefits of DORA Compliance

1. **Improved Cybersecurity Framework**
    - DORA enhances the cybersecurity resilience of financial institutions by requiring a unified approach to managing ICT risks, which minimizes potential disruptions and enhances recovery efforts.
2. **Harmonized Standards Across the EU**
    - By harmonizing cybersecurity practices, DORA ensures that all financial entities within the EU operate under consistent and standardized guidelines, promoting cross-border cooperation.
3. **Better Trust and Reputation**

- DORA compliance fosters greater public confidence in the financial sector, ensuring that institutions can handle cybersecurity incidents effectively and transparently.

4. **Stronger Third-Party Risk Management**
   - DORA's emphasis on third-party oversight reduces vulnerabilities introduced by external service providers, enhancing overall organizational security.

Strategic Considerations for Financial Entities

- **Executive-Level Accountability**: DORA mandates that executive leadership take responsibility for digital resilience, ensuring that all cybersecurity decisions are aligned with organizational objectives.
- **Cross-Departmental Collaboration**: Successful DORA compliance requires coordination across various departments, including IT, legal, risk management, and compliance teams.
- **Continuous Improvement**: DORA's focus on testing, monitoring, and resilience ensures that institutions remain adaptable and responsive to the ever-changing digital landscape.

Conclusion

The **Digital Operational Resilience Act (DORA)** is a vital regulation aimed at strengthening the digital security of the EU's financial sector. It ensures that financial entities can withstand cyberattacks and recover from digital disruptions. By following the compliance audit guide and aligning organizational practices with DORA's requirements, financial institutions can enhance their digital resilience, improve operational continuity, and build trust among stakeholders.

APPENDIX Q

SOC Reports

Overview of SOC Reports

SOC (**System and Organization Controls**) reports are independent assessments conducted under the AICPA's **SSAE 18** standards, designed to evaluate how service organizations manage and safeguard data. These reports focus on critical areas such as security, availability, processing integrity, confidentiality, and privacy—particularly important for organizations handling sensitive customer data.

SOC Reports are typically categorized into three main types:

SOC 1: Financial Reporting Controls

Purpose:

SOC 1 reports assess an organization's internal controls over **financial reporting**. These reports are especially relevant to companies that directly impact their client's financial reports.

Key Features:

- Focus on Internal Control over Financial Reporting (ICFR)

- Commonly used for payroll processors, financial SaaS platforms, and other organizations impacting financial reporting
- Requested by auditors of user organizations to assess financial risk

Types:

- **Type I**: Describes the controls in place at a **specific point in time**
- **Type II**: Tests and validates the operating effectiveness of controls over a **period of time** (usually 6–12 months)

SOC 2: Trust Services Criteria (TSC)

Purpose:

SOC 2 reports evaluate how organizations manage **data security** across five **Trust Services Criteria**: security, availability, processing integrity, confidentiality, and privacy.

Key Features:

- Based on the **COSO framework** and **Trust Services Criteria**
- Highly customizable, focusing on selected principles such as **Security Only** or the **full TSC**
- Relevant for tech companies, cloud providers, SaaS platforms, and others storing and processing sensitive data

Types:

- **Type I**: Assesses the design of controls at a **specific point in time**

- **Type II:** Evaluates the **operating effectiveness** of the controls over a defined period of time

SOC 3: Public-Facing Summary of SOC 2

Purpose:

SOC 3 reports are simplified public versions of the SOC 2 reports. These provide a high-level overview of the **SOC 2** findings for public consumption, without disclosing sensitive control details.

Key Features:

- Same criteria as SOC 2 but includes no detailed descriptions or test results
- Primarily used for marketing, trust-building, and external brand credibility
- Unrestricted distribution, ideal for posting on websites or sharing with the public

Comparison Table

Feature	SOC 1	SOC 2	SOC 3
Focus	Financial reporting controls	Trust Services Criteria (TSC)	Summary of SOC 2 findings
Audience	User auditors, internal teams	Customers, partners, regulators	General public
Detail Level	High (controls + tests)	High (controls + tests)	Low (summary only)
Distribution	Restricted	Restricted	Unrestricted

Type I / II Options	Yes	Yes	No
Use Case	Financial audit support	Security & compliance assurance	Brand trust & transparency

Strategic Notes for GRC Leaders

- **SOC 1**: Aligns well with **SOX compliance** and financial audits, particularly focusing on **internal controls over financial reporting** (ICFR).
- **SOC 2 Type II**: Often mapped to broader security frameworks like **ISO 27001, NIST CSF**, or **PCI DSS**, offering security assurance beyond financial controls.
- **SOC 3**: Provides a public-facing summary of SOC 2 findings, ideal for **external trust signals** and enhancing transparency without disclosing sensitive audit details.

APPENDIX R

SOX (Sarbanes-Oxley Act of 2002)

Introduction to SOX

Signed into Law: July 30, 2002

Primary Sponsors: Senator Paul Sarbanes and Representative Michael Oxley

Catalyst:

The **Sarbanes-Oxley Act (SOX)** was enacted in response to the financial scandals of the early 2000s, most notably **Enron, WorldCom,** and **Tyco.** These scandals, marked by fraudulent financial reporting and ineffective internal controls, led to massive investor losses and public distrust.

Objective of SOX

SOX aims to restore public confidence in financial markets by improving the accuracy, transparency, and accountability of corporate financial disclosures.

Key Provisions and Sections

Section 302 – Corporate Responsibility for Financial Reports

- Requires **CEOs and CFOs** to personally certify the accuracy of financial statements
- Holds executives accountable for the effectiveness of **internal controls**

Section 404 – Management Assessment of Internal Controls

- Mandates annual reports assessing **internal controls** over financial reporting (ICFR)
- Requires **external auditors** to attest to management's assessment of controls
- This is one of the most resource-intensive sections and involves substantial compliance efforts.
- **Section 802 – Criminal Penalties**
- Imposes **fines and jail time** for altering or destroying financial records
- Sets **retention requirements** for audit documentation (minimum **7 years**)

Section 906 – Certification of Financial Reports

- Adds criminal penalties for submitting **false certifications** knowingly

Applicability of SOX

Who Must Comply?

- **Public Companies** listed in the U.S. (SEC registrants)
- **Foreign Companies** listed on U.S. exchanges

- **Accounting Firms** auditing public companies
- **Private Companies** may adopt SOX-like controls when preparing for an **IPO** or **M&A**

Organizational Impact

- **Finance & Accounting:** Must implement strong **internal controls** over financial reporting (ICFR).
- **IT & Security:** Must ensure **data integrity, access management, change control,** and **audit trails** are maintained for financial systems.
- **Audit & GRC Teams:** Must coordinate annual **SOX audits, control testing,** and executive-level reporting.

Integration with Other Frameworks

- **SOX Section 404** often overlaps with:
- **COSO** Internal Control Framework (used for designing and assessing controls)
- **COBIT** (for IT governance and control mapping)
- **ISO 27001 / NIST SP 800-53** (for technical controls supporting financial systems)

Strategic Considerations for GRC Leaders

- **SOX Compliance** is not limited to finance; it requires **cross-functional collaboration** between **IT, security, legal, and audit teams.**

- **Automation** and **continuous control monitoring** are becoming more common to reduce audit fatigue and improve assurance.
- **SOX readiness** is critical for **IPO-bound companies** and those undergoing **M&A due diligence.**

APPENDIX S

FedRAMP

Introduction to FedRAMP

The **Federal Risk and Authorization Management Program (FedRAMP)**, established in **2011**, is a critical component of the **Office of Management and Budget (OMB)** and was codified by the **FedRAMP Authorization Act of 2022**. Its primary mission is to ensure that cloud service providers (CSPs) meet stringent cybersecurity standards before handling federal data. This framework standardizes security assessments, authorizations, and continuous monitoring for cloud services used by federal agencies.

Development and Governance of FedRAMP

Key Entities Involved:

- **FedRAMP PMO (Program Management Office)**: Operates under the **General Services Administration (GSA)**, managing the authorization process and repository of cloud services.
- **FedRAMP Board**: Responsible for overseeing the program's performance and policy evolution, replacing the **Joint Authorization Board (JAB)**.

- **Authorizing Agencies:** Federal entities sponsor CSPs through the FedRAMP process, ensuring cloud providers meet required security standards.

FedRAMP Authorization Paths

FedRAMP offers two paths for authorization based on the level of impact and the type of entity:

- **Agency Authorization:** A single federal agency sponsors the CSP for authorization.
- **FedRAMP Board Authorization (formerly JAB):** A multi-agency authorization for **high-impact systems**, which require broader oversight.

Security Baselines in FedRAMP

FedRAMP uses the **NIST SP 800-53** security controls and applies them across three distinct impact levels:

Impact Level	Data Sensitivity	Example Use Case
Low	Public data	Public-facing websites
Moderate	Controlled Unclassified Information (CUI)	HR, financial systems
High	Mission-critical or national security	Law enforcement, healthcare

Applicability to Federal Agencies

Mandatory Use:

- **Per OMB guidance,** all **executive federal agencies** are required to use FedRAMP to validate the security of cloud services they procure.
- **FedRAMP applies** when cloud services create, collect, process, store, or maintain federal information.
- **Scope of Applicability:**
- Cloud services that are not **explicitly excluded** (e.g., social media platforms, search engines, etc.), will be subject to FedRAMP.
- Services must operate within a **shared responsibility model** for security and compliance.

Benefits of FedRAMP for Agencies

1. **Risk Consistency:**
    - Provides a uniform security posture across federal agencies, ensuring consistent and secure cloud procurement processes.
2. **Procurement Efficiency:**
    - Streamlines procurement by offering a FedRAMP Marketplace, where agencies can easily access pre-authorized cloud services.

3. **Continuous Monitoring:**

   - FedRAMP enables **ongoing assurance** of cloud security controls, ensuring that agencies stay ahead of evolving cybersecurity threats.

Strategic Notes for GRC Leaders

- **Interoperability with NIST SP 800-53:** FedRAMP aligns closely with **NIST SP 800-53**, making it compatible with other federal compliance frameworks.
- **Third-party Compliance:** Even if contractors or CSPs are not explicitly mentioned in contracts, agencies must ensure they meet **FedRAMP requirements.**
- **FedRAMP Moderate:** This is often used as a baseline for compliance with **DFARS 252.204-7012** in defense contracts.

APPENDIX T

Standard Network Ports and Protocols

Overview:

In networking, **ports** act as logical endpoints for communication, identified by numbers ranging from **0 to 65535**. A **protocol** defines the rules for data exchange between systems. The most commonly used transport protocols include **TCP** (Transmission Control Protocol), **UDP** (User Datagram Protocol), and others such as **AASCTP/DCCP**, which are used in specialized applications.

Well-Known Ports and Their Protocols

The **IANA (Internet Assigned Numbers Authority**) assigns **ports 0-1023** to commonly used services across systems:

The table below outlines the most common ports and their associated protocols, detailing the primary functions and security implications of each.

Port Number	Protocol	Service	Description	Security Considerations
20	**TCP**	**FTP Data**	File Transfer Protocol (data channel)	Ensure encryption of sensitive data during transfer.
21	**TCP**	**FTP**	File Transfer Protocol (control channel)	FTP is inherently insecure. Use **SFTP** or **FTPS** for secure transfers.
22	**TCP**	**SSH/SCP/SFTP**	Secure Shell, secure file transfer	Use strong authentication methods (e.g., multi-factor authentication) for enhanced security.
23	**TCP**	**Telnet**	Remote login (unencrypted)	Telnet is unencrypted and vulnerable. Replace with **SSH** for secure communication.
25	**TCP**	**SMTP**	Email routing between servers	Ensure proper email filtering to prevent spam and phishing attacks.
53	**TCP/UDP**	**DNS**	Domain Name System	Implement DNS security extensions (**DNSSEC**) to protect against DNS spoofing.
67	**UDP**	**DHCP**	DHCP server port	Ensure DHCP security to prevent unauthorized

				devices from connecting.
68	**UDP**	**DHCP**	DHCP client port	Restrict DHCP requests to trusted clients only to prevent rogue devices.
69	**UDP**	**TFTP**	Trivial File Transfer Protocol	Use only in trusted, secure environments, and replace with **SFTP** where possible.
80	**TCP**	**HTTP**	Web traffic (unencrypted)	Transition to **HTTPS** to secure all web traffic and prevent man-in-the-middle attacks.
110	**TCP**	**POP3**	Email retrieval	**POP3S** is recommended to ensure encrypted email retrieval.
143	**TCP**	**IMAP**	Email retrieval (advanced)	Implement **IMAPS** for encrypted email retrieval.
161	**UDP**	**SNMP**	Network monitoring and management	Use **SNMPv3** with authentication and encryption for secure network monitoring.
443	**TCP**	**HTTPS**	Secure web traffic	Ensure SSL/TLS certificates are properly configured and updated.

445	TCP	SMB	Windows file sharing	Ensure **SMB v3** is used, and disable older versions (**SMB v1**) due to known vulnerabilities.
993	TCP	IMAPS	Secure IMAP	Always use **IMAPS** to ensure encrypted email retrieval.
995	TCP	POP3S	Secure POP3	Ensure **POP3S** is enabled for secure email retrieval over SSL/TLS.
3306	TCP	MySQL	Database access	Use strong encryption for database connections, and enforce access control.
3389	TCP	RDP	Remote Desktop Protocol	Use **RDP Gateway** and enforce strong authentication and encryption for secure access.
5432	TCP	PostgreSQL	Database access	Secure PostgreSQL connections using **SSL/TLS** encryption.

Governance and Security Implications

Firewall Configuration:

- Only necessary ports should be **open** in the firewall, while others should be **blocked** or monitored.

Vulnerability Management:

- Legacy services, like **Telnet** and **FTP**, should be replaced with more secure alternatives (e.g., **SSH** or **SFTP**).

Audit Readiness:

- Port usage should align with **documented system roles** and **security policies** to maintain audit readiness.

Threat Detection:

- Unusual port activity may indicate **lateral movement** or **exfiltration attempts** within the network.

APPENDIX U

Artificial Intelligence (AI)

Artificial Intelligence (AI) is the simulation of human intelligence processes in machines programmed to think, learn, and make decisions autonomously. At its core, AI enables systems to perform tasks that typically require human cognition, such as language understanding, pattern recognition, problem-solving, and adaptation to new information.

Core Capabilities of AI

AI encompasses several key capabilities that empower it to perform complex tasks. These include:

- **Machine Learning** (ML): This refers to algorithms that enable systems to learn from data and improve their performance over time without explicit programming. It is at the heart of predictive analytics, helping businesses forecast trends and behaviors.
- **Natural Language Processing** (NLP): This allows machines to understand, interpret, and generate human language, thereby enhancing communication between humans and computers. It's crucial for chatbots, voice assistants, and language translation systems.

- **Computer Vision:** With the ability to analyze and interpret visual information, AI can assist in applications ranging from facial recognition to self-driving cars.
- **Expert Systems:** These are rule-based systems that emulate human expertise to make decisions in specific domains, offering automated advice based on set criteria.
- **Robotics & Automation:** AI-powered systems that automate physical tasks, ranging from manufacturing robots to digital process automation, significantly improving efficiency and accuracy.

Types of AI

AI can be categorized into various types based on its capability:

Type	Description	Example
Narrow AI	Designed for a specific task or a narrow domain.	Spam filters, facial recognition
General AI	Hypothetical AI capable of performing any intellectual task a human can.	Not yet achieved
Generative AI	AI that can create new content, such as text, images, or code.	ChatGPT, Copilot, DALL·E

AI in Enterprise Context

AI is becoming increasingly pivotal in regulated industries, where it is leveraged to improve operational efficiency and compliance:

- **Automating Compliance Checks**: AI can quickly assess and automate compliance workflows, easing the burden of documentation and reporting for regulations like GDPR or HIPAA.
- **Enhancing Threat Detection**: AI systems can detect anomalies in vast datasets at scale, identifying potential threats faster and more accurately than traditional methods.
- **Generating Audit-Ready Reports**: AI can generate structured reports that help businesses prepare for audits, saving significant time and reducing human error.
- **Interpreting Regulatory Texts**: Using NLP, AI can interpret complex regulatory language, helping organizations map controls across frameworks such as ISO 27001, PCI DSS, and NIST.

Governance Implications

- While AI offers immense promise, it also presents new governance challenges. For AI to be effectively integrated into your operations, these key aspects need attention:
- **Transparency**: It's essential that AI's decision-making process is explainable. This transparency ensures accountability and mitigates risks associated with bias or unintended outcomes.
- **Accountability**: Clear ownership must be defined for AI systems. Organizations should identify who is responsible for the outputs and actions driven by AI, especially when things go wrong.

- **Ethics & Bias:** AI systems must be designed to avoid biases—whether related to race, gender, or other attributes. Ethical considerations should guide the training data used for AI models, ensuring fairness and non-discrimination.
- **Regulatory Compliance:** As AI becomes more ubiquitous, regulators are implementing laws (e.g., the **EU AI Act** and **NIS2**) that enforce stringent guidelines on its use, especially in critical systems.

AI in Vulnerability Management

AI is transforming how organizations detect, prioritize, and remediate vulnerabilities, driving efficiency and predictive intelligence:

1. **Detection & Threat Intelligence**
    - **Automated Scanning:** AI-powered scanning tools can analyze large amounts of data, identifying vulnerabilities and zero-day threats faster than traditional tools.
    - **Behavioral Analysis:** Machine learning models help identify abnormal patterns indicative of attacks, even when traditional signatures aren't available.
    - **Threat Intelligence Correlation:** By aggregating threat intelligence from various sources, AI can provide a comprehensive view, reducing false positives and enhancing decision-making.
2. **Prioritization & Risk Scoring**
    - **Context-Aware Risk Models:** AI takes into account the criticality of assets, exploitability, and business impact to assign more precise risk scores to vulnerabilities.

- **Predictive Analytics:** AI can predict which vulnerabilities are likely to be exploited, based on historical patterns and attacker behaviors, helping organizations allocate resources more effectively.

3. **Remediation & Automation**

   - **Automated Patch Recommendations:** AI-driven tools can suggest the most effective remediation strategies, including patching, configuration changes, or implementing compensating controls.
   - **Workflow Orchestration:** Integration with ITSM tools automates ticket creation, escalations, and verification, improving response time and reducing manual errors.

AI in IT Compliance

AI is revolutionizing compliance management, particularly in organizations with complex, multi-framework environments. Here's how:

1. **Intelligent Mapping & Harmonization**

   - **Control Mapping Engines:** AI can align and harmonize controls across various frameworks (ISO 27001, NIST, GDPR, PCI DSS), enabling a more streamlined compliance process.
   - **Dynamic Gap Analysis:** AI continuously monitors the effectiveness of controls and automatically identifies gaps or misalignments in compliance frameworks.
   - **Evidence Collection & Audit Readiness**

- **Automated Evidence Gathering**: AI bots collect relevant logs, screenshots, and configurations from systems to generate audit-ready reports, saving time and reducing the risk of missing critical evidence.
- **NLP**: AI uses natural language processing to extract relevant clauses from policies, procedures, and regulatory texts, matching them with control requirements automatically.

2. **Compliance Dashboards & Reporting**

- **Executive Summaries**: AI translates complex, technical compliance data into business-friendly insights, helping executives make informed decisions about risk management.
- **Continuous Monitoring**: AI-enabled dashboards provide real-time visibility into compliance status, tracking changes in regulations and audit trails.
- **Challenges & Considerations**
- While AI brings tremendous potential, it also introduces specific governance and ethical concerns:
- **Model Transparency**: Some AI systems operate as "black boxes," making it difficult to trace how decisions are made. This lack of transparency complicates accountability and auditability.
- **Bias & Data Quality**: AI models rely on data, and if that data is flawed or biased, it can skew risk assessments or compliance interpretations.

- **Regulatory Scrutiny**: As regulations around AI usage tighten, organizations must stay up-to-date on evolving laws (e.g., the **EU AI Act, NIS2**) to ensure compliance.

Strategic Recommendations

For GRC leaders looking to integrate AI into their cybersecurity and compliance functions, the following initiatives are essential:

Initiative	Description
AI Governance Framework	Establish policies that promote ethical AI use, ensure model validation, and guarantee auditability of AI decisions.
Compliance-Aware AI Models	Train AI models using regulatory language and control libraries to ensure alignment with compliance standards.
Human-in-the-Loop Oversight	Ensure critical decisions (e.g., risk acceptance, control failures) always involve human review and oversight.
Cross-Framework Dashboards	Leverage AI to create unified views across frameworks (ISO, NIST, PCI, GDPR) to enable executive-level reporting and strategic alignment.

INDEX

1. Access Control

Access control is a core cybersecurity mechanism that determines who or what can access digital systems, data, or resources, and what actions they are allowed to perform. It ensures that only authorized users, devices, or processes interact with protected assets according to predefined policies.

Purpose and Significance

Access control supports three key principles:

- **Confidentiality:** Prevents unauthorized disclosure of sensitive information.
- **Integrity:** Ensures data is not altered by unauthorized entities.
- **Availability:** Maintains system functionality for legitimate users while restricting malicious access.

Why it matters:

- Prevents data breaches and insider threats.
- Enforces **least privilege** and **Zero Trust** principles.
- Helps meet compliance standards (e.g., GDPR, HIPAA, PCI DSS).

Core Components

Component	Description
Authentication	Verifies identity (e.g., passwords, biometrics, MFA)
Authorization	Determines access rights and privileges
Access Enforcement	Applies rules via firewalls, IAM systems, or ACLs
Audit & Monitoring	Tracks access events for accountability and anomaly detection

Common Access Control Models

Model	Description
Discretionary Access Control (DAC)	Resource owners assign permissions (e.g., file-level ACLs)
Mandatory Access Control (MAC)	Central authority enforces access based on classification labels
Role-Based Access Control (RBAC)	Access granted based on user roles and responsibilities
Attribute-Based Access Control (ABAC)	Decisions based on user, resource, and environmental attributes

Implementation Levels

- **Network Level:** Firewalls, VPNs, NAC systems
- **Application Level:** IAM platforms, SSO, session controls
- **Physical Level:** Badge systems, biometric scanners

2. **Attestation of Compliance (AoC)**

Attestation of Compliance (AoC) is a formal document certifying an organization's adherence to the **Payment Card Industry Data Security Standard (PCI DSS)**. It serves as proof of compliance and is required by acquirers, banks, and partners in the payment ecosystem.

Purpose and Significance

- Demonstrates PCI DSS compliance for entities handling cardholder data.
- Required for business relationships involving payment processing.
- Supports regulatory and contractual obligations to maintain secure environments.

Key Elements of an AoC

Element	**Description**
Entity Identification	Name and details of the organization being assessed
Validation Method	Indicates whether a Self-Assessment Questionnaire (SAQ) or QSA audit was used
Compliance Status	Confirms if all PCI DSS requirements were met
Scope of Assessment	Defines systems, environments, and processes included
Signature and Date	Signed by an authorized officer and/or Qualified Security Assessor (QSA)

AoC vs. RoC

Document	Purpose	Audience	Depth
AoC	Certifies compliance	External stakeholders	Summary
RoC	Details assessment findings	Internal/external auditors	Comprehensive

3. Application Programming Interface (API)

An **API (Application Programming Interface)** is a set of protocols, routines, and tools that enables software applications to communicate with each other. It acts as a bridge between systems, allowing one application to request services or data from another.

Think of an API as a **restaurant waiter:** it takes your order (request), delivers it to the kitchen (server), and brings back your meal (response).

API Applications

In Cybersecurity:

- **Identity & Access Management (IAM):** Integrates authentication services like OAuth, SAML, OpenID Connect.
- **SIEM & SOC Tools:** Enables log ingestion, alerting, and threat intelligence sharing.
- **Vulnerability Management:** Connects scanners to ticketing systems for automated remediation.
- **Zero Trust Architectures:** Enforces policy-based access controls across microservices and endpoints.

In Enterprise Systems:

- **Cloud Integration:** Connects SaaS platforms (e.g., Salesforce, Microsoft 365) with internal systems.
- **Data Exchange:** Facilitates secure data sharing between departments, vendors, and regulators.
- **Automation & Orchestration:** Drives workflows in DevSecOps, GRC platforms, and compliance dashboards.

Types of APIs

Type	Description
REST	Lightweight, HTTP-based, widely used in web services
SOAP	XML-based, strict protocol, used in legacy enterprise systems
GraphQL	Flexible querying, popular in modern app development
Webhooks	Event-driven callbacks for real-time updates

4. Attack Surface

An **attack surface** refers to all the points—digital, physical, and human—where an unauthorized actor could attempt to access or extract data from a system, network, or application. A larger attack surface means more opportunities for exploitation.

Think of it as the **"doors and windows" of your digital house**—some locked, some forgotten, some wide open.

Components of an Attack Surface

Category	Description	Examples
Digital	Software and network entry points	APIs, open ports, misconfigured cloud assets, outdated software, shadow IT
Physical	Hardware endpoints and physical access	USB ports, discarded devices, unlocked workstations, badge access
Social Engineering	Human vulnerabilities	Phishing, pretexting, impersonation, insider threats

4. Attack Surface vs. Attack Vector

- **Attack Surface:** The full set of possible entry points where a system, network, or application could be exploited.
- **Attack Vector:** The specific method used to exploit one of those points, such as phishing, malware, or credential stuffing.

Applicability in GRC and Audit

Governance:

- Identify and categorize attack surfaces across business units.
- Align mitigation strategies with enterprise risk appetite.

Risk Management:

- Prioritize high-risk areas (e.g., internet-facing APIs, legacy systems).
- Map attack surfaces to threat models and likelihood-impact matrices.

Compliance & Audit:

- Maintain inventories of attack surfaces to validate control coverage (e.g., NIST SP 800-53 RA-5, CA-7).
- Demonstrate continuous monitoring and risk reduction efforts in audit reports.

How to Reduce the Attack Surface

- **Asset Inventory:** Maintain real-time visibility of all digital and physical assets.
- **Patch Management:** Regularly update software and firmware.
- **Access Controls:** Enforce least privilege and multi-factor authentication (MFA).
- **Decommissioning:** Securely retire unused systems and credentials.
- **Attack Surface Management (ASM):** Use continuous discovery and monitoring tools.

5. Business Impact Analysis (BIA)

A **Business Impact Analysis (BIA)** identifies and evaluates the potential effects of disruptions on an organization's critical business functions. It helps determine operational and financial impacts from events like cyberattacks, natural disasters, or supply chain failures, guiding recovery strategies.

In simple terms: *"What happens if this function fails—and how quickly must it be restored?"*

Key Objectives

- Identify mission-critical processes.
- Quantify downtime impacts (e.g., revenue loss, regulatory penalties).
- Define **Recovery Time Objectives (RTOs)** and **Recovery Point Objectives (RPOs)**.
- Prioritize resource allocation for continuity and recovery.
- Support risk assessments and business continuity planning.

Core Components

Component	**Description**
Process Inventory	Catalog of business functions and dependencies
Impact Assessment	Financial, operational, reputational consequences
Recovery Requirements	RTO, RPO, staffing, technology, third-party dependencies
Criticality Ranking	Tiered prioritization of functions for restoration
Scenario Modeling	Simulations of disruptions (e.g., ransomware, data center outage)

Applicability in GRC Programs

Governance:

- Align continuity planning with strategic objectives.
- Inform board-level risk appetite and investment decisions.

Risk Management:

- Support threat modeling and impact-based risk scoring.
- Enhance resilience metrics and Key Risk Indicators (KRIs).

Compliance & Audit:

- Required or recommended by standards such as ISO 22301, NIST SP 800-34, FFIEC, and HIPAA.
- Demonstrates preparedness in regulatory reviews and third-party assessments.

Integration with Other Frameworks

Framework	BIA Role
ISO 22301	Foundation for Business Continuity Management System (BCMS)
NIST SP 800-34	Core input for contingency planning
HIPAA	Required for contingency planning under Security Rule
FFIEC	Integral to IT risk and continuity assessments in financial institutions

6. BYOD (Bring Your Own Device)

BYOD is a policy allowing employees, contractors, or authorized users to use personal devices—smartphones, laptops, tablets, USB drives—to access corporate networks, data, and applications.

This shifts device ownership from the organization to the individual while maintaining access to enterprise resources.

Benefits

- **Cost Efficiency:** Reduces hardware procurement and maintenance costs.
- **User Productivity:** Employees work on familiar devices, improving speed and comfort.
- **Flexibility:** Supports remote and hybrid work models.
- **Risks**
- **Data Leakage:** Personal devices may lack enterprise-grade security.
- **Shadow IT:** Unmonitored apps or services may bypass governance controls.
- **Compliance Exposure:** Challenges in enforcing regulations like GDPR, HIPAA, or PCI DSS.

Security Controls

Control Area	Examples
Authentication	Enforce MFA, device certificates
Device Management	Use MDM/MAM tools to enforce encryption and remote wipe
Network Access	Segment BYOD traffic via VPN or NAC
Policy Enforcement	Acceptable use policies, onboarding/offboarding protocols

7. Chief Information Security Officer (CISO)

A **CISO** is a senior executive responsible for establishing and leading an organization's cybersecurity strategy, protecting digital assets, ensuring regulatory compliance, and maintaining resilience against cyber threats.

Core Responsibilities

Domain	Key Functions
Governance	Develop and enforce security policies, standards, and frameworks
Risk Management	Identify, assess, and mitigate cyber risks
Compliance	Ensure adherence to regulations (GDPR, HIPAA, PCI DSS, NIS2, DORA)
Incident Response	Lead detection, containment, and recovery from cyber incidents

Security Architecture	Oversee secure design of systems, networks, and applications
Awareness & Training	Promote a security-conscious culture across the organization
Reporting	Communicate risk posture and metrics to executive leadership and the board

Strategic Significance

- **Board-Level Influence:** CISOs often report to the CEO or board, reflecting cybersecurity's strategic importance.
- **GRC Integration:** CISOs drive governance, risk, and compliance programs across business units.
- **Digital Resilience:** Ensure continuity and recovery during cyber disruptions.

8. Cloud Computing

The **cloud** is a global network of remote servers hosted in data centers that store, manage, and process data over the internet. Instead of relying on local infrastructure, users and organizations access computing resources, applications, and storage on demand.

The cloud is scalable, flexible, and accessible from anywhere, forming the backbone of modern digital services.

Key Characteristics

Feature	Description
Remote Access	Data and applications are accessed via the internet
Scalability	Resources can be scaled up or down based on demand
Cost Efficiency	Reduces need for physical infrastructure and maintenance
Flexibility	Supports remote work, global collaboration, and rapid deployment
Security & Compliance	Built-in controls, encryption, and compliance options (ISO 27001, GDPR, HIPAA)

Cloud Models

Model	Description
Public Cloud	Services offered over the internet (e.g., AWS, Azure, Google Cloud)
Private Cloud	Dedicated infrastructure for a single organization, often for regulatory or security needs
Hybrid Cloud	Combines public and private clouds for flexibility and control
Multi-Cloud	Uses multiple providers to avoid vendor lock-in and optimize performance

Common Cloud Services

- **IaaS (Infrastructure as a Service):** Virtual machines, storage, networking (e.g., AWS EC2, Azure).
- **PaaS (Platform as a Service):** Development platforms and tools (e.g., Google App Engine).
- **SaaS (Software as a Service):** Applications accessed via browser (e.g., Microsoft 365, Salesforce).
- **Real-World Examples**
- **Dropbox / Google Drive:** Cloud storage
- **Netflix / Spotify:** Streaming via cloud-hosted content
- **Gmail / Outlook:** Cloud-based email
- **Salesforce / SAP:** Enterprise SaaS platforms

9. CMDB (Configuration Management Database)

A **CMDB** is a centralized repository storing information about an organization's IT assets (Configuration Items, or CIs) and their relationships. It is key to IT Service Management (ITSM) and supports **change management, incident response, and impact analysis.**

What CMDB Tracks

Configuration Item (CI)	Examples
Hardware	Servers, routers, laptops, mobile devices
Software	Applications, OS, licenses
Network Components	Firewalls, switches, load balancers
Virtual Assets	VMs, containers, cloud instances
Facilities & People	Data centers, support staff, vendors

Each CI includes:

- Unique ID
- Owner
- Status
- Relationships
- Change history

Applicability

- **Risk Management:** Identify critical assets, prioritize vulnerabilities.
- **Compliance & Audit:** Trace changes, support ISO 27001, NIST SP 800-53, HIPAA, PCI DSS.
- **Incident Response:** Map upstream/downstream impacts for faster root cause analysis.

- **Change Management:** Assess risk before changes, reduce disruptions.

CMDB vs ITAM

Aspect	CMDB	ITAM
Focus	Relationships & dependencies	Inventory & lifecycle
Granularity	Tracks interconnections	Tracks ownership & value
Use Case	Impact analysis, change control	Procurement, depreciation, disposal

10. COSO ERM

COSO ERM is the Enterprise Risk Management framework by COSO, aligning risk management with strategy to enable **proactive, value-driven governance.**

Framework Overview

- Latest Version: 2017
- Structure: 5 components, 20 principles

Core Components

Component	Description
Governance & Culture	Tone at the top, risk awareness
Strategy & Objective-Setting	Align risk with mission and performance goals

Performance	Identify and respond to risks affecting objectives
Review & Revision	Evaluate and improve ERM effectiveness
Info, Communication & Reporting	Ensure timely, relevant risk data flows

Applicability

- **Strategic Risk Alignment:** Integrates cybersecurity, compliance, operational risk with business strategy.
- **Audit & Assurance:** Benchmark for internal and external audits.
- **Regulatory Compliance:** Supports GDPR, HIPAA, DORA, NIS2, financial regulations.

11. CyberScope

1. **CyberScope by NetAlly – Handheld Analyzer**
    - **Purpose:** Edge network vulnerability assessment.
    - **Capabilities:** Endpoint/network discovery, Nmap vulnerability scans, device classification, rogue detection, compliance testing.
    - **Use Case:** Field engineers, SOC teams, OT/IoT-heavy environments.
2. **CyberScope Platform for FISMA Reporting (U.S. Federal)**
    - **Purpose:** Federal agencies submit FISMA metrics to OMB.

- **Functions:** Quarterly/annual reporting, metrics aligned with NIST CSF, used by CIOs/CISOs/privacy officers.

12. Data Masking

Data Masking hides sensitive data using realistic fake values to protect privacy while keeping data usable.

Use Cases

- Software testing
- Analytics & research
- Third-party sharing
- Employee training

Types

Type	Description	Use Case
Static	Alters data at rest	Dev/test, data sharing
Dynamic	Masks data in real-time	Production systems
Deterministic	Consistent replacements	Referential integrity
On-the-Fly	During migration/ETL	Cloud migration/data pipelines
Tokenization	Non-sensitive tokens	Payment systems, PCI DSS

Techniques: Character shuffling, substitution, nulling, encryption, format-preserving masking

Regulatory Alignment: GDPR, HIPAA, PCI DSS, CCPA

13. DDoS (Distributed Denial-of-Service)

A **DDoS attack** overwhelms servers, services, or networks with massive traffic from multiple compromised devices.

How it Works

- Malware infects devices to form a botnet.
- Botnet floods target with traffic.
- Target becomes slow/unavailable.

Types

Type	Description
Volumetric	Flood bandwidth (e.g., UDP floods)
Protocol	Exploit protocol weaknesses (e.g., SYN floods)
Application Layer	Fake requests to web apps (e.g., HTTP floods)
Fragmentation	Incomplete packets to exhaust resources

Applicability

- **Risk Management:** Downtime, data loss, reputational damage; often used in ransomware/hacktivism.
- **Compliance & Governance:** PCI DSS, NIS2, ISO 27001 (network security).
- **Incident Response:** Real-time detection, filtering, failover; tools like Cloudflare, Akamai, AWS Shield, Arbor Networks.

14. DevOps

Definition:

DevOps combines **Development (Dev)** and **Operations (Ops)** to unify teams, processes, and tools for faster, reliable software delivery. It's both a **cultural** and **operational shift**, breaking silos between developers and IT operations.

Core Principles:

Principle	**Description**
Collaboration	Dev and Ops teams share responsibilities across the lifecycle
Automation	Testing, deployment, and monitoring are automated
Continuous Integration (CI)	Code changes integrated and tested frequently
Continuous Delivery (CD)	Software released safely and quickly
Infrastructure as Code (IaC)	Infrastructure managed via code for scalability
Monitoring & Feedback	Continuous observation to improve systems

GRC Relevance:

- **Governance:** Aligns with Agile governance and ISO 27001 (A.12.1.2, A.14.2.7)
- **Risk Management:** Reduces deployment risks and improves resilience

- **Compliance:** DevSecOps supports PCI DSS, HIPAA, NIST SP 800-53, DORA

Lifecycle Phases:

Phase	Activities
Plan	Define features, create backlog, align goals
Develop	Code, test, review, integrate collaboratively
Deliver	Deploy applications & infrastructure reliably
Operate	Monitor systems, gather feedback, optimize performance

DevOps Metrics (DORA):

- Deployment Frequency → Agility
- Lead Time for Changes → Speed of delivery
- Change Failure Rate → Stability
- Failed Deployment Recovery Time → Resilience

15. DLP (Data Loss Prevention)

Definition:

DLP detects, monitors, and prevents unauthorized data access or transmission. It protects **data in motion, at rest, and in use** across endpoints, networks, and cloud.

Objectives:

- Prevent breaches and leaks
- Protect PII, PHI, financial data, IP

- Regulatory compliance: GDPR, HIPAA, PCI DSS, CCPA
- Monitor user behavior

Types:

Type	Description
Network DLP	Monitors/filter traffic (email, web, files)
Endpoint DLP	Controls laptops, desktops, mobile devices
Cloud DLP	Protects SaaS/IaaS data
Storage DLP	Scans databases & file repositories

Key Features:

- Data classification and tagging
- Policy enforcement
- Real-time alerts & blocking
- Encryption & redaction
- Audit logging

GRC Applicability:

- Governance → Policies & standards
- Risk Management → Insider threats, high-risk flows
- Compliance → GDPR Art. 32, HIPAA Security Rule, PCI DSS Req. 3, CCPA

16. Encryption

Definition:

Transforms readable data (plaintext) into **ciphertext** using algorithms, accessible only with the correct key. Ensures **confidentiality, integrity, and authentication.**

Process:

1. Plaintext → Original data
2. Algorithm → Mathematical transformation
3. Key → Encryption/decryption string
4. Ciphertext → Scrambled data
5. Decryption → Restores plaintext

Types:

Type	Description
Symmetric	Same key for encrypt/decrypt (fast, key sharing risky)
Asymmetric	Public key encrypts, private key decrypts (secure communication)
Hashing	One-way integrity checks (e.g., SHA-256)

GRC Role:

- Governance → ISO 27001 A.10, secure policy enforcement
- Risk Management → Protects data in transit & at rest
- Compliance → HIPAA, PCI DSS, GDPR, CCPA

Use Cases:

- Secure emails, files, databases
- Cloud storage & backups
- Online transactions
- Remote work confidentiality

17. Endpoints

Definition:

Any device connecting to a network. Endpoints are entry points for data and cyber threats.

Examples:

Category	Devices
User Devices	Laptops, desktops, smartphones, tablets
Servers	File, web, database servers
IoT Devices	Cameras, smart speakers, medical devices
Virtual Assets	VMs, containers, cloud workloads
POS Systems	Retail terminals, kiosks, payment devices

Importance:

- Attack Surface → First compromise point for phishing, malware, ransomware
- Security → Antivirus, EDR, MDM, ZTNA
- Compliance → HIPAA, PCI DSS, ISO 27001, NIST SP 800-53

18. Firewalls

Definition:

Network security devices/software controlling traffic based on rules. Acts as a **digital bouncer**, permitting safe traffic and blocking threats.

Types:

Type	**Description**
Packet Filtering	Basic IP, port, protocol inspection
Stateful Inspection	Tracks connections & context
Proxy Firewall	Intercepts traffic; adds anonymity
Next-Gen Firewall	Deep packet inspection, IPS, app control
Web Application Firewall (WAF)	Protects web apps (SQLi, XSS)

Key Functions:

- Traffic filtering
- Threat prevention
- Policy enforcement
- Monitoring & logging

Compliance Relevance:

- PCI DSS → Req.1 firewall config
- HIPAA → ePHI technical safeguards
- ISO 27001 → A.13.1 network security
- NIST SP 800-53 → AC-4, SC-7 boundary protection
- DORA/NIS2 → Network segmentation, threat mitigation

19. FISMA (Federal Information Security Modernization Act)

Overview:

FISMA is a U.S. federal law that creates a framework for securing government information systems. Originally enacted in 2002 and updated in 2014, it strengthens oversight and modernizes federal cybersecurity practices.

Purpose and Scope:

- Requires federal agencies to implement agency-wide information security programs.
- Annual reviews to ensure effective risk management.
- Oversight by OMB, operational support from DHS.

Key Security Objectives:

- **Confidentiality:** Protect sensitive data from unauthorized access.
- **Integrity:** Ensure data remains accurate and unaltered.

- **Availability:** Guarantee reliable access to information when needed.

Compliance Requirements:

- Annual security reviews and risk assessments.
- Continuous system monitoring.
- Adherence to NIST standards, especially NIST SP 800-37 (certification & accreditation).

2014 Reform Highlights:

- DHS's role codified in administering security policies.
- Clarified OMB oversight authority.
- Streamlined reporting and introduced new breach notification requirements.

20. FortiSIEM

Overview:

FortiSIEM is Fortinet's next-gen Security Information and Event Management platform that unifies visibility, analytics, automation, and threat intelligence across IT and OT environments.

Key Capabilities:

- **Unified Event Correlation:** Combines logs, flow data, SNMP traps, cloud services, and third-party tools.
- **User & Entity Behavior Analytics (UEBA):** Detects anomalies using machine learning.

- **Built-in SOAR Automation:** Automates incident response with pre-built playbooks.
- **Advanced Threat Detection:** Maps to MITRE ATT&CK framework, integrates FortiGuard intelligence.
- **CMDB:** Monitors asset health and performance automatically.
- **Cloud & Hybrid Deployment:** Works across AWS, Azure, GCP, and on-prem.

AI-Powered Features:

- **FortiAI-Assist:** Provides GenAI-driven insights for analysts.
- **Customizable ML Models:** Tailors detection logic for specific environments.

Ideal Use Cases:

- Enterprises needing unified SOC/NOC operations.
- MSSPs managing multi-tenant environments.
- Real-time threat detection and compliance reporting.

21. Hashing

Overview:

Hashing converts input data into a fixed-length string using a hash function. Output is a hash value or digest.

How Hashing Works:

- Hash function processes input into a unique, fixed-size output.
- Small changes in input drastically alter the hash.

Key Properties:

- Deterministic: Same input → same hash.
- Irreversible: Original data cannot be reconstructed.
- Collision-resistant: Hard to find two inputs producing the same hash.
- Fast computation: Efficient for large datasets.

Use Cases:

- Password storage.
- Data integrity verification.
- Digital signatures.
- Blockchain linking.

Hashing vs. Encryption:

Feature	Hashing	Encryption
Direction	One-way	Two-way (encrypt/decrypt)
Purpose	Integrity, verification	Confidentiality
Reversible	No	Yes (with key)
Use Case	Passwords, checksums, signatures	Secure communication, data privacy

22. HMOs (Health Maintenance Organizations)

Overview:

HMO is a type of health insurance plan offering care via a network of providers at reduced rates.

Key Features:

- Network-based care: Must use in-network providers.
- Primary Care Physician (PCP) coordinates care.
- Specialist referrals required.
- Typically lower premiums and out-of-pocket costs.

Pros:

- Predictable costs, lower premiums.
- Coordinated care through PCP.
- Emphasis on preventive care.

Cons:

- Limited provider choice.
- Referral requirements can delay care.
- No out-of-network coverage (except emergencies).

HMO vs. PPO Comparison:

Feature	HMO	PPO
Network Restrictions	In-network only	Flexible
Specialist Access	Requires referral	No referral needed
Cost	Lower premiums	Higher premiums
Care Coordination	Through PCP	Self-managed

23. IAM (Identity and Access Management)

Overview:

IAM frameworks manage digital identities and control access to resources, ensuring correct access at the right times.

Core Functions:

- Authentication (passwords, biometrics, MFA).
- Authorization (roles, policies, permissions).
- User lifecycle management (creation, updates, deactivation).
- Audit & monitoring of access events.

Key Components:

- IAM Policies
- Role-Based Access Control (RBAC)
- Single Sign-On (SSO)
- Multi-Factor Authentication (MFA)

Strategic Importance:

- Supports Zero Trust Architecture.
- Ensures regulatory compliance (HIPAA, GDPR, NIST).
- Prevents credential-based breaches (~80% of cyberattacks).

Example (Hospital System):

- Doctors access patient records.
- Admin staff manage appointments but not medical data.
- IAM ensures secure, precise access.

24. IDS (Intrusion Detection System)

Overview:

IDS monitors network/system activity for malicious behavior, policy violations, or unauthorized access.

Core Functions:

- Traffic monitoring
- Threat detection (signatures or anomalies)
- Alerting security teams
- Logging for forensic analysis

Types of IDS:

- **NIDS:** Network-based, monitors entire network.
- **HIDS:** Host-based, monitors individual devices.

Detection Methods:

- Signature-based
- Anomaly-based
- Reputation-based

IDS vs. IPS:

Feature	IDS	IPS
Role	Detects & alerts	Detects & blocks
Action	Passive	Active
Placement	Inline or passive	Inline

Importance:

- Improves visibility.
- Supports compliance (NIST, ISO 27001, HIPAA).
- Early detection of insider and external threats.

25. IoT (Internet of Things)

Overview:

IoT is a network of connected devices with sensors and software that communicate autonomously over the Internet or private networks.

Core Concepts:

- Smart connectivity
- Autonomous communication

- Unique identifiers for each device

Examples:

Category	Devices
Consumer IoT	Smart thermostats, trackers, speakers
Industrial IoT	Factory sensors, predictive maintenance tools
Healthcare IoT	Remote patient monitors, wearable ECG devices
Smart Cities	Traffic sensors, smart lighting, waste management

How It Works:

1. Sensors gather data (temperature, motion, location).
2. Connectivity transmits data via Wi-Fi, Bluetooth, Zigbee, or cellular.
3. Processing occurs locally (edge) or in the cloud.
4. Actions taken automatically or via user input.

Risks & Challenges:

- Security vulnerabilities from weak authentication or outdated firmware.
- Privacy concerns.
- Interoperability across platforms and protocols.

Why It Matters:

- Enables predictive maintenance in manufacturing.
- Real-time logistics tracking.

- Personalized healthcare solutions.
- Energy-efficient smart homes.

26. IPS (Intrusion Prevention System)

An IPS actively monitors network traffic to detect and block threats in real time. Unlike IDS, it is deployed inline and can act immediately.

Core Functions:

- Threat detection (signature-based or anomaly-based)
- Automated blocking/quarantining of malicious traffic
- Logging & alerts for security teams
- Policy enforcement

Detection Techniques:

- Signature-based: Known attack patterns
- Anomaly-based: Deviations from normal behavior
- Vulnerability-facing signatures: Potential exploits

IPS vs IDS:

Feature	IDS	IPS
Role	Detects & alerts	Detects & blocks
Deployment	Passive	Inline
Action	Manual or delayed	Real-time, automated

Usage: Enterprise edges, data centers, NGFWs, cloud environments.

Benefits: Stops attacks proactively, reduces false positives, supports compliance (NIST, ISO 27001, PCI DSS, HIPAA).

27. ISO 31000

An international standard providing guidelines for effective risk management, adaptable to organizations of all types and sizes.

Key Components:

- Principles: Integrated, value-creating, decision-supporting risk management
- Framework: Structure for embedding risk management
- Process: Identify, analyze, evaluate, treat, monitor, communicate

Applicability:

- Sector-neutral, scalable, non-certifiable (guidance standard)

Benefits:

- Aligns risk management with strategic goals
- Improves decision-making and resilience
- Supports regulatory compliance

ISO 31000 vs COSO ERM:

Feature	ISO 31000	COSO ERM
Origin	International	U.S.-based
Focus	Principles & process	Governance & internal control

Certifiable	No	No

28. ISO/IEC 27001:2022

Global standard for Information Security Management Systems (ISMS), providing a framework to protect sensitive information.

Purpose:

- Establish, implement, maintain, and improve ISMS
- Systematic risk identification & treatment
- Align security with business and legal requirements

Key Updates (2022):

- Clauses refined (4–10), Clause 6.3 added for change management
- Annex A controls reduced from 114 → 93; 11 new controls added (e.g., threat intelligence, data masking)
- Controls grouped into Organizational, People, Physical, Technological

Benefits:

- Enhances cyber resilience and risk awareness
- Ensures regulatory compliance (GDPR, HIPAA, NIS2)
- Builds trust and improves operational efficiency

Users: Organizations handling sensitive data wanting better IP protection, compliance, and governance.

29. ITSM (IT Service Management)

Strategic approach to managing IT services to align IT operations with business needs.

Core Functions:

- Service Request Management, Incident Management, Problem Management
- Change Management, Configuration Management

Frameworks: ITIL, COBIT, ISO/IEC 20000

Benefits:

- Improves service quality & user satisfaction
- Enhances efficiency & compliance
- Enables scalable IT operations & digital transformation

ITSM vs ITIL:

Concept	ITSM	ITIL
Definition	"What" of managing IT services	"How" via best practices
Scope	Broad IT service delivery	Framework within ITSM
Certification	ISO/IEC 20000	ITIL Foundation, Practitioner, etc.

30. Log4j

Open-source Java logging framework by Apache for recording application events.

Key Features:

- Flexible logging outputs (JSON, XML, plain text)
- Appenders for files, DB, email, or remote servers
- Filters & Layouts for custom logging
- Plugin architecture & multi-API support

31. Log4Shell

Critical zero-day vulnerability in Log4j 2 (Dec 2021) enabling remote code execution via log message injection.

Dangers:

- Remote code execution without authentication
- Affected millions globally
- Exploitable through simple text inputs
- CVSS 10/10 (highest severity)

Mitigation:

- Upgrade to Log4j ≥2.17.1
- Disable risky features (JNDI lookups)
- Monitor logs & use runtime protections

Lesson: Emphasizes secure logging practices, rapid patching, and software supply chain security.

32. Man-in-the-Middle (MITM) Attack

A Man-in-the-Middle (MITM) attack occurs when an attacker secretly intercepts and potentially alters communications between two parties who think they are directly communicating.

How It Works

1. **Interception** – Attacker positions between two entities (e.g., user and website).
2. **Eavesdropping** – Captures sensitive data like passwords or financial info.
3. **Manipulation** – Alters data before sending it along, appearing legitimate.

Common MITM Types

Type	Description
Wi-Fi Eavesdropping	Fake hotspots trick users into exposing data
Email Hijacking	Impersonates trusted contacts to steal credentials or redirect funds
Session Hijacking	Steals session tokens to impersonate users
SSL Stripping	Downgrades HTTPS to HTTP to intercept unencrypted traffic
DNS Spoofing	Redirects users to malicious sites by corrupting DNS responses

Prevention

- Use **end-to-end encryption** (HTTPS, TLS)
- Avoid public Wi-Fi or use a **VPN**
- Enable **multi-factor authentication**
- Keep software and browsers updated

- Monitor **certificate anomalies**

Real-World Impact

- Banking credential theft
- Financial transaction hijacking
- Corporate espionage
- Exploitation of IoT devices

33. **MFA (Multi-Factor Authentication)**

MFA requires two or more independent credentials to verify identity, protecting accounts even if passwords are compromised.

Authentication Factors

- **Something you know** – password, PIN
- **Something you have** – smartphone, hardware token
- **Something you are** – fingerprint, facial scan

Common MFA Methods

Method	**Description**
SMS/Email OTP	One-time codes via text/email
Authenticator Apps	Time-based codes (Google/Microsoft Authenticator)
Push Notifications	Approve logins via mobile app
Biometrics	Fingerprint or facial recognition
Hardware Tokens	Physical devices like YubiKey or smart cards

Importance

- Prevents credential-based attacks (phishing, password spraying)
- Reduces account takeover risk
- Supports compliance (HIPAA, PCI DSS, NIST)
- Makes accounts **99% less likely to be hacked** (CISA)

MFA vs. 2FA

Term	Definition
2FA	Exactly two factors
MFA	Two or more factors

34. Misconfiguration in Cybersecurity

Misconfiguration occurs when software, hardware, or cloud settings are incorrect or insecure, exposing systems to risk.

Impact

- Sensitive data exposure
- Unauthorized access
- Malware installation or lateral movement
- Full system compromise

Common Examples

Type	Description
Default Credentials	Factory usernames/passwords (admin/admin)
Open Ports	Unrestricted SSH, RDP, database access
Unpatched Systems	Missing security updates
Overly Permissive Access	Excess privileges for users/apps
Verbose Error Messages	Reveals internal system info
Misconfigured Cloud Storage	Public S3 buckets or blobs
Disabled Security Features	Firewalls, antivirus, encryption turned off

Prevention

- Secure configuration baselines
- Automated configuration management
- Regular audits and vulnerability scans
- Least privilege principle
- Monitor configuration drift and enforce change control

Cloud and third-party environments are particularly prone to misconfigurations.

35. Missing Patch

A **missing patch** is a security update or fix not applied to a system, leaving it vulnerable.

Why Patches Matter

- Fix security vulnerabilities
- Resolve bugs/performance issues
- Ensure compliance (PCI DSS, HIPAA, NIST)
- Maintain system stability

Causes

- Poor patch management
- Disabled automatic updates
- Unsupported legacy systems
- Failed installations
- Delayed testing in production

Detection Tools

- PowerShell: Get-WindowsUpdate –IsInstalled $false
- Patch management platforms (e.g., ManageEngine Endpoint Central)
- RMM/SIEM dashboards

Best Practices

- Centralized patch management
- Regular scanning and updates
- Prioritize critical patches
- Maintain rollback plans

- Monitor compliance across endpoints

36. MTTR (Mean Time to Repair)

MTTR measures the average time to restore a system after failure.

Formula

MTTR=Total Repair TimeNumber of Repairs\text{MTTR} =\frac{\text{Total Repair Time}}{\text{Number of Repairs}}MTTR=Number of Repair sTotal Repair Time

Example: 3 failures totaling 6 hours → MTTR = 2 hours

Importance

- Indicates operational resilience
- Measures incident response efficiency
- Supports SLA compliance
- Guides resource planning and training

Related Metrics

Metric	Definition
MTTR	Mean Time to Repair/Recovery
MTBF	Mean Time Between Failures
MTTF	Mean Time to Failure (non-repairable)
MTTA	Mean Time to Acknowledge (detection speed)

37. NIST

NIST (National Institute of Standards and Technology) is a U.S. federal agency promoting innovation and standards to improve economic security and quality of life.

Role in Cybersecurity

- NIST Cybersecurity Framework (CSF)
- Special Publications (e.g., SP 800-53) for security and privacy controls
- Supports risk management, identity & access management, zero trust, and supply chain security

Other Areas

- Quantum science
- Artificial intelligence
- Bioscience and healthcare IT
- Manufacturing/metrology
- Energy and communications

38. On-Prem (On-Premises)

On-prem refers to software, data, or IT infrastructure hosted locally within an organization's physical facilities instead of the cloud or third-party data centers.

Key Characteristics

- **Local Hosting:** Servers physically on-site.

- **Full Control:** Organization manages hardware, software, and data.
- **Security & Compliance:** Preferred in regulated industries.
- **Upfront Costs:** Significant investment in hardware and licensing.

On-Prem vs. Cloud

Feature	On-Premises	Cloud-Based (SaaS)
Hosting Location	Organization's data center	Vendor-managed remote servers
Control	Full control	Limited, vendor-managed
Cost Structure	High upfront costs	Subscription-based, lower entry
Scalability	Limited	Highly scalable
Maintenance	Internal IT	Cloud provider

Use Cases

- Banks requiring data residency
- Healthcare under HIPAA
- Government with classified data
- Enterprises with legacy or custom systems

39. Phishing

Phishing is a cyberattack using deceptive communications to trick users into revealing sensitive information.

How It Works

- Impersonates trusted entities
- Creates urgency or fear
- Redirects to fake websites

Common Types

Type	Description
Email Phishing	Mass emails from fake sources
Spear Phishing	Targeted attacks using personal info
Smishing	SMS-based phishing
Vishing	Voice call phishing
Clone Phishing	Replicates legitimate emails

Protection Tips

- Verify senders before clicking links
- Use MFA
- Check URLs carefully
- Keep software updated
- Report suspicious messages

40. Policy

A policy is a formal set of principles guiding decision-making within an organization.

Characteristics

- **Intentional:** Created for specific goals
- **Guiding:** Steers actions
- **Consistent:** Uniform application
- **Authoritative:** Approved by leadership

Examples & Types

Domain	Example
Corporate	Data privacy, remote work
Government	Immigration, fiscal policy
Security/GRC	Access control, incident response
Insurance	Life, auto policies

Policy vs. Law vs. Procedure

Term	Purpose	Enforceability
Policy	Guides decisions	Internal enforcement
Law	Mandates or prohibits	Legally binding
Procedure	Step-by-step instructions	Operational enforcement

41. Qualys VMDR

VMDR = Vulnerability Management, Detection, and Response. Cloud-native solution for identifying, prioritizing, and remediating vulnerabilities.

Core Capabilities

- Asset Discovery: Finds all devices, including unmanaged
- Vulnerability Assessment: Scans for known & zero-day threats
- Risk Prioritization: TruRisk™ scoring
- Automated Remediation: Patch & mitigate risks
- Threat Detection: AI-driven malware detection
- Dashboard & Reporting: Custom insights

Key Concepts

- TruRisk Score, Asset Criticality Score (ACS), Qualys Detection Score (QDS), Qualys Query Language (QQL)

Benefits

- Reduce patch time by up to 60%
- Continuous attack surface visibility
- Compliance with PCI DSS, HIPAA, ISO 27001, NIST
- ITSM integration

42. RAID (Redundant Array of Independent Disks)

Data storage technology combining multiple drives for performance, redundancy, or capacity.

Popular RAID Levels

RAID	Description	Fault Toler-ance	Use Case
RAID 0	Striping for speed	None	Video editing, gaming
RAID 1	Mirroring	1 drive	Critical storage
RAID 5	Striping + parity	1 drive	Servers
RAID 6	Striping + double parity	2 drives	High availability
RAID 10	RAID 1+0	Multiple	Enterprise performance & safety

RAID Controllers

- Hardware RAID: Dedicated card, faster
- Software RAID: OS-managed, cost-effective
- Firmware RAID: BIOS-based, hybrid

43. RBAC (Role-Based Access Control)

Access control model that grants permissions based on roles instead of individuals.

Core Concepts

- **Role:** Job function (e.g., HR Manager)
- **Permission:** Action allowed (read/write/delete)
- **User:** Assigned to role(s)
- **Session:** User-role-permission mapping during login

Example

- HR Manager: view/edit employee records
- Intern: view public documents

Benefits

- Simplifies administration
- Improves security, prevents privilege creep
- Supports least privilege
- Easier audits

RBAC in Practice

- Azure RBAC: Cloud resource access
- Enterprise ERP/CRM/GRC systems
- Compliance with ISO 27001, NIST SP 800-53, HIPAA

44. RFID (Radio-Frequency Identification)

Definition: RFID is a wireless technology that identifies, tracks, and manages objects using radio waves. Unlike barcodes, it does not require a direct line of sight.

Components:

- **RFID Tag:** Chip + antenna storing data (e.g., unique ID)
- **RFID Reader:** Emits radio waves and receives tag signals
- **Backend System:** Software that processes and stores collected data

Types of Tags:

Type	Power Source	Range	Use Case
Passive	Powered by reader's signal	Up to ~10m	Inventory, ID cards, retail
Active	Battery-powered	Up to ~100m+	Vehicle tracking, asset monitoring
Semi-passive	Battery-powered, uses reader signal	Medium	Environmental sensing

Applications:

- Retail: Inventory tracking, theft prevention
- Healthcare: Patient ID, equipment tracking
- Logistics: Package tracking, warehouse automation
- Security: Access cards, passport chips
- Animal ID: Pet microchips

Security Considerations:

- Unauthorized scanning (skimming)
- Data leakage if tags aren't encrypted
- Tracking without consent
- **Mitigation:** Encryption, RFID-blocking wallets, access controls

- **45. RMF (Risk Management Framework)**

Definition: RMF is a structured process by NIST to manage cybersecurity, privacy, and supply chain risks throughout the system development life cycle.

Purpose: Integrates security/privacy controls, risk-based decisions, continuous monitoring, and compliance (e.g., FISMA).

7 RMF Steps:

Step	**Description**
Prepare	Establish context, priorities, and readiness
Catego-rize	Define system and assess impact (CIA: Confidentiality, Integrity, Availability)
Select	Choose baseline security controls based on risk
Imple-ment	Deploy and document controls
Assess	Evaluate control effectiveness
Authorize	Decision to operate based on risk
Monitor	Continuous tracking of controls and emerging risks

Importance:

- Systematic risk management
- Regulatory compliance (FISMA, HIPAA)
- Secure system authorization (ATO)
- Continuous improvement and accountability

46. ROC Templates (Report on Compliance)

Definition: Standardized templates for Qualified Security Assessors (QSAs) to document PCI DSS compliance.

Purpose:

- Document assessment findings
- Provide evidence of compliance/non-compliance
- Support Attestation of Compliance (AOC)
- Ensure consistency

PCI DSS v4.0.1 Highlights:

- Improved usability, reduced redundancy
- Aligns with updated PCI DSS requirements
- Includes major sections, appendices, and sample templates

Typical Sections:

Section	Description
Executive Summary	Overview of scope, methodology, findings
Detailed Findings	Requirement-by-requirement evidence
Validation Summary	Final compliance status and assessor judgment
Appendices	Diagrams, data flow maps, supplemental validation

47. RPO (Recovery Point Objective)

Definition: Maximum acceptable data loss (measured in time) after a disruption.

Example: RPO = 1 hour → Back up or replicate data at least every hour; maximum data loss = 1 hour

RPO vs. RTO:

Metric	Definition	Focus
RPO	Maximum tolerable data loss	Data integrity
RTO	Maximum tolerable downtime	System availability

Importance:

- Defines backup frequency
- Guides storage/replication strategy
- Supports critical vs. non-critical data classification
- Aligns with business impact analysis & compliance

48. RTO (Recovery Time Objective)

Definition: Maximum allowable downtime before causing unacceptable business impact.

Example: RTO = 2 hours → Operations must be restored within 2 hours

RTO vs. RPO:

Metric	Focus	Example
RTO	Time to restore operations	"System back online in 2 hours"
RPO	Acceptable data loss	"Up to 15 minutes of data loss allowed"

Importance:

- Drives infrastructure resilience (hot vs. cold sites)
- Guides incident response playbooks
- Prioritizes critical systems
- Supports cost-benefit analysis for recovery investments

49. SaaS (Software as a Service)

SaaS is a cloud computing model where software is delivered over the internet on demand, usually via subscription. Users access it through a web browser, while the provider manages infrastructure, updates, and maintenance.

Key Features

- **Hosted by provider:** No local installation needed.
- **Access via browser:** Available anytime, anywhere.
- **Subscription-based:** Monthly or annual payments, often tiered.
- **Automatic updates:** New features and patches rolled out seamlessly.
- **Scalable:** Usage can adjust according to business needs.

Examples

Category	SaaS Product	Purpose
Communication	Slack, Zoom	Messaging and video conferencing
Productivity	Microsoft 365, Google Workspace	Email, documents, spreadsheets
Design	Canva, Figma	Graphic and UI design
CRM	Salesforce, HubSpot	Customer relationship management
AI Services	Azure AI, OpenAI API	Natural language, vision, decision-making

Benefits

- Lower upfront costs
- Faster deployment
- Reduced IT overhead
- Seamless collaboration
- Built-in security and compliance

Challenges

- Limited customization
- Vendor lock-in risks
- Data privacy and control concerns
- Integration with legacy systems

50. SDLC (Software Development Life Cycle)

SDLC is a structured process for designing, developing, testing, and deploying software, ensuring it is delivered on time, within budget, and aligned with user requirements.

Common Phases

Phase	Description
Planning	Define scope, resources, timeline, feasibility
Requirements Analysis	Gather functional and non-functional requirements
Design	Architecture, UI/UX, technical specifications
Development	Writing code and building the software
Testing	Validate functionality, performance, security
Deployment	Release software to users
Maintenance	Monitor, patch, and enhance post-launch

Benefits

- Clear project roadmap
- Better risk management
- Improved stakeholder communication
- Higher software quality and customer satisfaction

51. SNMP (Simple Network Management Protocol)

SNMP is an application-layer protocol for network management and monitoring of devices across IP networks. It allows administrators to collect, organize, and sometimes modify device data.

Architecture

- **Manager (NMS):** Central system querying and controlling devices
- **Agent:** Software on a managed device responding to queries
- **MIB (Management Information Base):** Database of variables (CPU, memory, interfaces)

Operations

Operation	Purpose
GetRequest	Retrieve data from an agent
SetRequest	Modify a variable on an agent
GetNextRequest	Iterate through MIB variables
Trap	Unsolicited alert from agent to manager
Response	Agent's reply to manager

Versions

- **SNMPv1:** Original, basic functionality
- **SNMPv2c:** Improved performance, community-based security
- **SNMPv3:** Adds authentication, encryption, and access control

Importance

- Enables real-time network monitoring
- Supports automated alerts and fault detection
- Facilitates capacity planning and performance tuning
- Integrates with SIEMs and NMS platforms for enterprise visibility

52. SOAR (Security Orchestration, Automation, and Response)

SOAR is a cybersecurity framework that helps security teams **automate, coordinate, and streamline incident response**. It collects data from multiple sources, automates repetitive tasks, orchestrates workflows, and enables faster, more consistent threat responses.

Core Components

Component	Function
Orchestration	Integrates disparate security tools into unified workflows
Automation	Executes predefined actions without manual input
Response	Coordinates incident handling from alert to resolution
Case Management	Tracks incidents, investigations, and analyst actions

Benefits

- Reduces alert fatigue and manual workload
- Improves response time and consistency
- Enhances collaboration across security and IT teams
- Supports compliance and audit readiness

Example Use Case

A phishing alert arrives via SIEM:

1. Automatically enriches the alert with threat intelligence
2. Checks if the sender domain is malicious
3. Quarantines the email and blocks the sender
4. Opens a case and notifies the SOC analyst

53. SOC (Security Operations Center)

A SOC is a **centralized team or facility** responsible for monitoring, detecting, analyzing, and responding to cybersecurity threats in real time. It combines **people, processes, and technology** to protect digital assets.

Core Functions

Function	Description
Threat Monitoring	Continuously scans networks, endpoints, and cloud environments
Incident Detection	Uses SIEM, SOAR, and XDR tools to identify potential threats

Function	Description
Investigation & Analysis	Triages alerts, investigates root causes, and assesses impact
Response & Mitigation	Executes playbooks to contain and remediate threats
Threat Intelligence	Leverages internal and external data to anticipate attacks
Continuous Improvement	Refines processes, updates detection rules, adapts to new threats

Technologies Used

- **SIEM:** Aggregates and analyzes logs
- **SOAR:** Automates incident workflows
- **XDR:** Integrates telemetry across endpoints, networks, and cloud
- **Threat Intelligence Platforms:** Provide context on attacker behavior

SOC Models

Model	Description
Internal SOC	Operated in-house
MSSP	Outsourced to a third-party vendor
Hybrid SOC	Combines internal and external resources

Model	Description
GSOC	Coordinates security across multiple regions

Benefits

- Faster incident response
- Improved visibility across the attack surface
- Enhanced compliance (NIST, ISO 27001, HIPAA)
- Reduced business risk and downtime

54. SQL Injection (SQLi)

SQL Injection is a **web vulnerability** that allows attackers to manipulate database queries via unsanitized user input, potentially exposing sensitive data, modifying records, or gaining server control.

How It Works

- Occurs when user input is embedded in SQL queries without validation.
- Example:

  SELECT * FROM Users WHERE UserId = '105 OR 1=1';

  Here, OR 1=1 always evaluates true, returning all users instead of just one.

Common Types

Type	Description
In-band SQLi	Injects and retrieves data using the same channel
Error-based SQLi	Exploits database error messages to gain information

Union-based SQLi	Uses UNION operator to combine results from multiple queries
Blind SQLi	No visible output; infers behavior through timing or logic
Out-of-band SQLi	Uses alternate channels (DNS, HTTP) to extract data

Prevention

- Use parameterized queries (prepared statements)
- Sanitize and validate user input
- Apply least privilege access to databases
- Use web application firewalls (WAFs)
- Regularly test for vulnerabilities (Burp Suite, OWASP ZAP)

Real-World Impact

The 2019 **Capital One breach** exposed data of over 100 million customers due to a misconfigured web app vulnerable to SQLi.

55. SSL (Secure Sockets Layer)

SSL is a **cryptographic protocol** that secures internet communication by encrypting data between a user's browser and a web server. Although SSL has largely been replaced by TLS (Transport Layer Security), the term "SSL" is still widely used.

Key Features

Feature	Description
Encryption	Converts data into unreadable format to prevent eavesdropping
Authentication	Verifies the server's identity (and optionally the client)
Data Integrity	Ensures data hasn't been altered during transmission
HTTPS	Enables secure HTTP communication

How SSL Works

1. Handshake: **Browser and server exchange cryptographic keys and agree on encryption methods.**
2. Certificate Verification: **Server presents its SSL certificate; browser validates it.**
3. Session Key Generation: **A shared key is created for encrypting the session.**
4. Secure Communication: **All data is encrypted using the session key.**

Types of SSL Certificates

Type	Use Case
Domain Validation (DV)	Basic encryption; verifies domain ownership
Organization Validation (OV)	Confirms domain and organization identity

Extended Validation (EV)	Highest trust; shows company name in browser bar

Why SSL Matters

- Protects user privacy and sensitive data
- Builds trust with visitors
- Required for PCI DSS compliance
- Improves SEO rankings (Google favors HTTPS sites)

56. Syslog

Syslog is a **standard protocol** for collecting, storing, and forwarding log messages from devices and applications across a network. It's crucial for system monitoring, troubleshooting, and security auditing.

Key Components

Component	Role
Syslog Sender	Generates log messages (routers, servers)
Syslog Receiver	Collects and stores logs centrally
Syslog Message	Contains timestamp, severity, facility, message content

Message Structure

- **Facility code:** Source of the message (kernel, mail, auth, etc.)
- **Severity level:** 0 (Emergency) to 7 (Debug)
- **Timestamp & hostname**

- **Message content**

Example Syslog Message

<34>Oct 11 22:14:15 my host ss h d 12345]: Failed password for invalid user admin from 192.168.1.10 port 22

<34>: Encoded priority (facility + severity)

Oct 11 22:14:15: Timestamp

- My host: Hostname
- Ss h d[12345]: Process name & ID
- Message: Event description

Use Cases

- Security monitoring (failed logins)
- Troubleshooting (service crashes)
- Compliance auditing (PCI DSS, HIPAA)
- Performance tracking

Devices Using Syslog

- Routers, switches, firewalls
- Linux/Unix servers
- Printers, IoT devices
- Applications like Apache, MySQL

57. Threat

A **cybersecurity threat** is any event, actor, or circumstance that can exploit a vulnerability to harm systems, data, or digital assets. Threats can be **intentional** (hackers) or **unintentional** (human error).

Key Characteristics

Attribute	Description
Source	Hackers, insiders, nation-states, natural disasters
Intent	Often malicious: steal data, disrupt operations, extort money
Vector	Phishing, malware, misconfigurations, social engineering
Impact	Data breaches, financial loss, reputational damage, penalties

Common Types of Cybersecurity Threats

Threat Type	Description
Malware	Viruses, worms, ransomware, trojans
Phishing	Fraudulent messages to steal sensitive info
Social Engineering	Manipulation to bypass security
SQL Injection	Malicious SQL code to manipulate databases
Ransomware	Encrypts data; demands payment
Insider Threats	Employees misusing access
Zero-Day Exploits	Attacks on unpatched vulnerabilities
DDoS Attacks	Overloading systems to cause outages

Insights & Mitigation

- Threats evolve rapidly; dwell times can shrink to minutes.
- Social engineering is now a leading breach method.
- Mitigation strategies:
- Multi-layered defenses (firewalls, EDR, SIEM)
- Zero trust & least privilege access
- Security awareness training
- Patch systems & monitor anomalies
- Incident response planning

58. Three-Way Handshake

The **three-way handshake** establishes a reliable TCP connection between a client and server before data transfer begins.

Steps

1. **SYN (Synchronize):** Client sends SYN packet with a sequence number.
2. **SYN-ACK (Synchronize-Acknowledge):** Server acknowledges and sends its sequence number.
3. **ACK (Acknowledge):** Client confirms the server's number. Connection established.

Importance in Cybersecurity

- Ensures mutual readiness and authentication

- Prevents data loss or corruption
- Basis for secure protocols like HTTPS
- Helps detect SYN floods and spoofing attacks

Security Enhancements

- Use TLS/SSL to encrypt the handshake
- Firewalls to filter malicious SYN packets
- Monitor anomalous traffic

TCP vs UDP

Feature	TCP	UDP
Connection Type	Connection-oriented (handshake)	Connectionless (no handshake)
Reliability	High (ensures delivery & order)	Low (no guarantee)
Speed	Slower due to overhead	Faster
Data Transmission	Stream-based	Message-based
Header Size	20 bytes	8 bytes
Error Handling	Retransmission & checksums	Minimal (checksum only)
Flow Control	Yes	No
Ordering	Guaranteed	Not guaranteed

Use Cases	Web browsing, email, FTP, SSH	Streaming, gaming, DNS, VoIP

When to Use

- TCP: Reliability & integrity critical (banking, file transfer)
- UDP: Speed & low latency prioritized (live video, gaming)

Security Considerations

- TCP commonly used for secure communications (TLS/SSL)
- UDP more vulnerable to spoofing; requires rate limiting & authentication

59. TLS (Transport Layer Security)

TLS is the **successor to SSL** and encrypts internet communications, ensuring privacy, authentication, and data integrity.

Key Functions

Function	Description
Encryption	Protects data from unauthorized access
Authentication	Verifies identity of communicating parties
Integrity	Ensures data isn't altered during transmission

How TLS Works

1. Handshake to agree on encryption algorithms and keys
2. Exchange and verify digital certificates
3. Generate a shared session key for encryption

TLS in Action

- HTTPS websites
- Email encryption (STARTTLS)
- VPNs, VoIP, messaging apps

TLS Certificates

- Issued by trusted Certificate Authorities (CAs)
- Enable encrypted sessions and prove website identity

60. Tokenization

Definition: Replacing sensitive data or real-world assets with a non-sensitive digital token that keeps essential information without exposing the original data.

a) In Data Security

- **Purpose:** Protect sensitive information (credit cards, personal identifiers) and ensure compliance (PCI DSS, HIPAA, GDPR, CCPA).
- **How it works:** Sensitive value → randomly generated token stored in a secure vault.

- **Use Cases:**
  - Payment processing (Apple Pay, Google Pay)
  - Healthcare data protection
  - Regulatory compliance

b) In Blockchain & Finance

- **Purpose:** Represent real-world assets (cash, bonds, real estate, equities) as blockchain tokens.

- **Process:**
  1. Custodian holds the asset.
  2. Blockchain token issued.
  3. Token circulates and is redeemable.

- **Benefits:** 24/7 access, fractional ownership, instant settlement, programmable finance.
- **Note:** Adoption is slow; JPMorgan reports ~$25B in tokenized assets.

c) In AI & NLP

- **Purpose:** Break text into tokens for machine processing.
- **Example:** "Hello world" → ["Hello", "world"] or ["Hel", "lo", "wor", "ld"]
- **Importance:** Foundational for large language models to understand and generate text.

61. VMs (Virtual Machines)

Definition: Software emulations of physical computers, running an OS and applications independently on a host machine via a hypervisor.

How VMs Work:

- Hypervisor allocates host CPU, RAM, and storage.
- Each VM runs its own OS independently.

- Can be cloned, paused, or deleted without affecting others.
- **Example:** 16 GB RAM server → two VMs with 8 GB RAM each.

Why Use VMs:

- Isolation: Sandboxed environments reduce cross-contamination risk.
- Efficiency: Multiple VMs on one physical server.
- Flexibility: Test different OSes/configurations.
- Disaster Recovery: Quick backup & restore.
- Cloud: Most services (AWS EC2, Azure VMs) use VMs.

VMs vs Containers:

Feature	Virtual Machines	Containers
Abstraction	Full OS & hardware	App & dependencies
Size	Heavier (GBs)	Lightweight (MBs)
Isolation	Strong	Moderate
Boot Time	Slower	Faster
Use Case	Multi-OS environments	Microservices, DevOps

62. Zero-Day

Definition: A software or hardware vulnerability unknown to the vendor, with no available patch—"zero days" to fix before exploitation.

Why Zero-Days Matter:

- Exploitable: Attackers can strike immediately.
- Hard to detect with traditional tools.
- High-value: Used in ransomware, cyberespionage, nation-state attacks.

Real-World Examples (2025):

- Google AI "Big Sleep" discovered a memory corruption zero-day in SQLite (CVE-2025-6965).
- Microsoft Security Copilot found GRUB2 bootloader flaws bypassing Secure Boot.
- Shows AI outpacing humans in discovering zero-days.
- **Management:**
- Bug bounty programs (e.g., Trend Micro ZDI) reward responsible disclosure.
- Threat intelligence monitors active exploitation.
- Virtual patching protects systems until official fixes are released.

www.ingramcontent.com/pod-product-compliance
Lightning Source LLC
LaVergne TN
LVHW050928210926
848482LV00013B/568